1996

LIBRARIES in the INFORMATION SOCIETY

Knowledge models for networked library services

Authors:
J.S. Mackenzie Owen and A. Wierck

European Commission, DG XIII-E/4

EUR 16905 EN

Published by the
EUROPEAN COMMISSION

Directorate-General XIII
ations, Information Market and Exploitation of Research

L-2920 Luxembourg

A great deal of additional information on the European Union is
available on the Internet. It can be accessed through the Europa server
(http://europa.eu.int)

Cataloguing data can be found at the end of this publication

Luxembourg: Office for Official Publications of the European Communities, 1996
ISBN 92-827-5838-9
© ECSC-EC-EAEC, Brussels • Luxembourg, 1996
Reproduction is authorized, except for commercial purposes, provided the source is acknowledged

Printed in Belgium

Preface

The 1993 Call for Proposals for the Libraries sector of the Telematics Programme was extremely rich in new ideas, both on the technology and service fronts. While many of these were specifically taken up by one or more of the 22 projects which followed, others were identified as important generic topics for further investigation in preparing the ground for future cooperative R&D work in networked library systems and services.

A number of studies under the general heading *Libraries in the Information Society* were therefore conducted over the next 24 months. In 1995, these led to four reports on:

- Artificial neural networks for information retrieval in a libraries context (EUR 16264);
- Chipcard use in libraries and information webs (EUR 16135);
- Business analysis of the library systems market in Europe (EUR 16121) and
- Library performance indicators and library management tools (EUR 16483).

The present study on Knowledge Models for Library Services is published as an addition to the series in parallel with another study report on Open Distance Learning in Public Libraries (EUR 16904). Both are considered as key contributions to the expanding role of public libraries in the networked environment.

The principal objective of the Knowledge Models study which follows has been to investigate the library's evolving role in the mediation process, combining collection-based resources with access to external documents of various types. In this context, it provides guidelines for librarians and library users wishing to make use of new models for acquisition, lending and reference based on integrated access to networked functions

The study was carried out over a ten month period up to November 1995 by John Mackenzie Owen of NBBI in the Netherlands.

Ian M. Pigott
Electronic Publishing and Libraries
April 1996

Management Summary

Objectives

This document is the final report on a study called 'Knowledge Models for Networked Library Services' commissioned by the European Commission. The study has three closely related objectives :

- To examine the library's evolving role in the knowledge mediation process in the light of scenarios combining existing collection-based procedures with access to external documents of various types.

- To review the specific need of users for services in the library environment with a view to increasing user interaction, improving the knowledge mediation potential and providing adequate help support at all levels.

- In the light of the above, to develop new library application models for acquisition, lending and reference incorporating integrated access to networked functions.

Background

Libraries, as a component of the information chain, act as a link between knowledge sources and users. They do this by performing three basic functions :

- Providing a 'window' on available knowledge through the library's holdings, catalogues, bibliographic materials, etc.

- Actually providing material to the users once they have decided what they need.

- Offering users various kinds of support related to the complex process of knowledge mediation and acquisition.

These three functions together constitute the 'knowledge mediation' function of the library.

Recent development in networking are creating significant changes in the way information is communicated between producers and users. These changes affect the role of libraries in many ways. They lead to a shift from collection-based libraries to an integrated combination of networked access and more traditional library services.

One of the most important questions now faced by libraries, is how to continue to provide added value as a knowledge mediator in the new networked world. An additional question is how to do this while at the same time preserving access to traditional, printed resources and providing services to users who are not connected to electronic networks.

The solution lies in enhancing existing library functions and in integrating traditional library approaches with state-of-the art information and communication technology. Libraries will therefore have to review the manner in which they communicate information and knowledge to their users. In future, tools for mediating knowledge will no longer be restricted to the catalogue but will also be based on other functions and tools offering organised access to wider information resources.

This report presents a general overview of libraries in the networked environment, a detailed analysis of issues related to the integration of networked services and traditional library functions, and a number of application model which demonstrate how integrated networked appendices with background material and a bibliography.

Conclusions

The main conclusion of this study is that libraries can continue to provide added value in the world of networked information in a way which is of interest to both information users and to publishers and their authors. The added value of networked library services is created through four important functions :

- *Resource selection* : the library acts as a selective filter which directs the user to relevant high quality resources. This function helps to solve the lack of selectivity and information overload experienced by network users.

- *Resource integration* : the library brings together a wide range of resource types, media, search tools etc. within an integrated, uniform environment. This function helps the user to focus on content rather than on media and methods in the knowledge seeking process.

- *User support* : the library offers a wide range of support mechanisms to help the user at all stages of the knowledge mediation process.

- *Intermediary between information producers and users* : the library acts as a linking mechanism between a large number of information producers (e.g. publishers) on the one side, and a large number of users on the other. This functions create a more efficient flow of information than when producers and users of information have to maintain direct bilateral relationships.

The study also makes clear, though, that there are many obstacles on the way to fully developed networked services. Important barriers include :

- The development stage and existing technical environment of libraries, which in many cases are insufficient to easily incorporate networked functions.

- The financial resources of libraries : integrating networked services in the library environment requires significant financial resources and investments in new systems, staff training, etc.

- Human factors such as user awareness and expectations, and staff awareness and skills. The library encounters two contrasting forces in this area. On the one hand, users and staff may take a conservative approach and not realise the need to develop towards networked services. On the other hand, enhanced network services are often expected from the library at a higher place than can be accomplished.

- Many other factors can create obstacles in individual cases. Examples include the lack of technical facilities at the national level, or the problem of language encountered in many European countries when entering the predominantly English-language world of networking.

Co-operation, both between libraries and between libraries and publishers, is found to be extremely important as a means to enhance networked library services. Co-operation between libraries can take the form of specialisation (e.g. domain based services) or centralised, national services. Co-operation between libraries and publishers can help to create effective means for distributing publications in electronic form.

The study demonstrates the feasibility of integrating networked functions with traditional library functions by mean of several *application models*. These models show what can be achieved in this area when full use is made of networking based on information and communication technology. The study also makes clear that a full stage of networked services can be reached through a development path based on the gradual introduction of networking and conversion to new systems and work methods.

Table of content

PART 1: OVERVIEW

1. Introduction 3
2. Scope 7
    2.1 Libraries and networks 7
    2.2 Electronic information resources 9
    2.3 Libraries and the Internet 11
3. Library functions 13
    3.1 Acquisition 13
    3.2 Cataloguing, indexing and reference services 16
    3.3 Consultation, lending and document delivery 21
    3.4 User support 24
    3.5 Digital libraries? 25
    3.6 Libraries in the networked environment 26

PART 2: CONCEPTUAL ANALYSIS

4. The basic functions of knowledge mediation 37
5. Acquiring information in the library 39
6. Organising the knowledge mediation function 41
7. Integrated resource discovery: strategies for reducing complexity 47
8. Maintaining the quality of knowledge mediation in the networked environment .. 53
    8.1 Quality of resources 53
    8.2 Quality of network access 56
9. Language issues in the networked environment 59
10. Bibliographic control of networked resources 63
    10.1 The expanded concept of bibliographic description 63
    10.2 Bibliographic description of networked resources 66
11. User support for knowledge mediation 73
    11.1 Support methods 73
    11.2 Support for networked knowledge mediation 75
12. Networked relations with publishers 81
    12.1 Electronic distribution from publishers to libraries 81
    12.2 Knowledge distribution strategies 83
    12.3 Library - publisher co-operation 85
13. Knowledge mediation and the library context 87
14. Key issues in knowledge mediation 89

PART 3: APPLICATION MODELS

15. Application models for networked library services..........................95
   15.1 Background factors...95
   15.2 An approach to application models 100
16. The Networked Library Model..101
   16.1 Components of the networked library system 101
   16.2 The user's view of the library 104
   16.3 Networked library functions..106
   16.4 Networked library systems 117
   16.5 Publisher relations 121
17. The Co-operative Network Model...123
   17.1 A client-server approach..123
   17.2 Domain-based and national services 124
   17.3 Integration at the client level 126
   17.4 Steps towards a co-operative network model 127
   17.5 The need for local services 128
18. The Knowledge Environment Model 129
   18.1 The public library as a knowledge environment............................129
   18.2 Characteristics of the public library.......................................129
   18.3 The networked public library functions....................................132
   18.4 Network aspects..133
19. A development path towards networked library services.....................135

20. Appendix 1: The global network infrastructure 141
   20.1 Background information on the Internet....................................143
   20.2 The technical infrastructure of the Internet 145
   20.3 Internet tools...147
   20.4 Standards 148
   20.5 Current developments..151
   20.6 Network resources 152

21. Appendix 2: Knowledge mediation concepts.................................159

22. Bibliography 171

List of figures

Figure 1: Types of networks 8

Figure 2: Access methods.. 23

Figure 3: Knowledge mediation 37

Figure 4: Resource discovery 39

Figure 5: Knowledge mediation decisions 42

Figure 6: Options for knowledge resources....................................... 44

Figure 7: USMARC Field 856 70

Figure 8: User decisions 79

Figure 9: Direct distribution to end-users... 83

Figure 10: Distribution through intermediaries................................. 84

Figure 11: Knowledge mediation activities....................................... 87

Figure 12: Components of the networked library system................... 103

Figure 13: The networked library system.. 117

Figure 14: The domain-based approach to co-operative library services 125

Figure 15: The national approach to co-operative library services 126

Figure 16: The Networked Public Library... 131

Figure 17: Network standards.. 149

Figure 18: A global network information system................................ 157

PART 1: OVERVIEW

1. Introduction

Libraries, as a component of the information chain, act as a link between knowledge sources and users. They do this by performing three basic functions:

- Providing a 'window' on available knowledge through the library's holdings, catalogues, bibliographic materials, etc. It is through this window that users can see what is available, and can choose information which is likely to fulfil their knowledge needs.

- Actually providing materials to the user once they have decided what they need.

- Offering users various kinds of support related to the complex process of knowledge mediation and acquisition.

These three functions together constitute the 'knowledge mediation' function of the library.

Although the service of libraries was at one time restricted to materials that were available on-site, developments in the library profession have expanded the view on available knowledge that the library can offer to the user. Bibliographies inform users about information that has been published, even when it is not physically available at the user's library. Union catalogues tell the user where, in other libraries, that information can be found. Inter-library lending systems allow the user to actually obtain the information from other locations. A major characteristic of the history of libraries is therefore that they have freed themselves from the constraint of the physical availability of documents and have been able to expand their knowledge mediation potential to an almost universal level.

Information technology and networking are important instruments for this development. They allow the library to access bibliographic information resources world-wide, to co-ordinate services with other libraries and to enter into transactions with libraries and information suppliers in order to deliver information to the user in an efficient way. Network technology also allows the user to access libraries and their knowledge sources, where and when he or she needs to. The range of library services available to users has increased in quantity and variety of choice, as well as in quality.

However, the further development of networking is also fundamentally changing the knowledge mediation function of libraries. Networks provide access to a wealth of reference materials, document sources and delivery services which are not necessarily stored in any library at all. For the end-user, the network acts like a huge repository of directly accessible information. Users therefore do not depend solely on libraries anymore to find out what knowledge is available, where it can be found, and for actually acquiring it. They increasingly have direct access to information that is available on or through the network. Libraries cannot depend on traditional library resources alone in performing their knowledge mediating function. They will have to expand their mediating function to the area of networked resources, services and tools.

In this context libraries have to define their future function as knowledge mediator. They have to redefine their role for users who have access to the full range of services on international networks. To what extent can libraries enhance their mediating role to provide added value to users? Do 'traditional' functions such as acquisition, cataloguing, indexing, lending and reference remain valid in the context of electronic, networked information? What kind of service and support do users require? These basic sets of questions have to be answered in order to give direction to change in libraries.

The Knowledge Models project

Networking offers libraries and library users new channels of access to information and new methods of working. A shift from a collection-based approach to an integrated combination of networked access and more traditional library services will bring about fundamental changes, both in user requirements and attitudes and in the work methods of the library. This will also have an impact on library systems.

Libraries will therefore have to review the manner in which they communicate information and knowledge to their users. In future, tools for mediating knowledge will no longer be restricted to the catalogue but will also be based on other functions and tools offering organised access to wider information resources.

In order to assist libraries in this process, the European Commission has set up a study project called 'Knowledge Models for Networked Library Services' with three closely related objectives:

- To examine the library's evolving role in the knowledge mediation process in the light of scenario's combining existing collection-based procedures with access to external documents of various types.

- To review the specific needs of users for services in the library environment with a view to increasing user interaction, improving the knowledge mediation potential and providing adequate help support at all levels.

- In the light of the above, to develop new library application models for acquisition, lending and reference incorporating integrated access to networked functions.

The project study has been conducted by NBBI, Project Bureau for Information Management in the Netherlands.

Structure of the report

This document is the final report of the study on knowledge models for networked library services. It consists of the following three main parts:

- Part 1 presents a general overview of the issues involved, based on desk research carried out for the study. The issues covered are:
    - Developments in the networked environment.
    - Library functions and services.
    - User requirements.

- Part 2 is a conceptual analysis of knowledge mediation in the context of networking. This part identifies and discusses a number of specific issues related to the integration of networked services and traditional library functions.

- Part 3 presents a number of application models which show how the concepts developed in part 2 could be implemented in order to achieve integrated network services in the library.

Additional material is contained in a number of appendices:
- Appendix 1 provides background information on the Internet as related to libraries.
- Appendix 2 is a schematic overview of concepts used for the analysis in part 2.
- Appendix 3 is a bibliography.

---

2. Scope

2.1 Libraries and networks

Since this study addresses networked library services, the concept of a network needs clarification. In fact, one can distinguish four types of networks which are relevant for libraries.

As indicated in the introduction, libraries have expanded the access to knowledge resources outside the user's own library by providing pointers in the form of bibliographies, reference journals, on-line databases, etc. This process has been further enhanced through union catalogues (describing the combined resources of a larger number of libraries) and through mechanisms for interlibrary lending and document delivery between libraries. A further step had been taken through the development of co-operative library networks which provide efficient electronic communication between libraries[1]. In fact, these *library specific networks* perform a dual function:

- For libraries as organisations, they provide a technical and organisational context for co-operation, resource sharing, electronic mail and distribution of bibliographic data and (electronic) documents.

- For end-users, they provide a mechanism for accessing other libraries than their own, e.g. for consulting OPACs and other databases in other libraries, and in some cases for making use of additional services.

A second type of network is the internal, *local library network*. Library systems are, at least in larger libraries, not isolated stand-alone computers. They consist of various components such as the on-line catalogue, administrative sub-systems (e.g. user registration, circulation, acquisitions), databases, CD-ROM-servers, and user terminals. These components are increasingly connected together through a 'local area network', i.e. a network through which the various components can communicate with each other and to which new components can be added.

A third type of network is the internal *network of the institution* to which the library belongs. A well known example of this is the campus network of academic institutions. This type of network provides communication between and access to various services

---

[1]   For an overview, see the LIBER directory edited by Dempsey (1992).

within the institution, e.g. the electronic mail system, the library, the computer centre, etc. The interface to these services is often provided in an integrated way, e.g. though a Campus Wide Information System (CWIS) which offers a hierarchical, menu-based entry point to the various sub-systems and services.

The fourth type of network is the (almost) *global information infrastructure* which has developed out of academic and government networks and is now referred to as the Internet. This basically consists of a mechanism which links other networks (e.g. institutional networks, internal library networks, co-operative library networks) together to form a single, universal information and communication network which provides access to any information system or service anywhere in the world, provided it is linked to the Internet. Access to these systems and services can be either unrestricted or controlled (e.g. through user registration and passwords).

Local library systems (e.g. OPACs), institutional networks and library specific co-operative networks are now increasingly being connected to the Internet, providing end-user access to union catalogues and individual OPACs. For end-users connected to the global information infrastructure, the distinction between library networks and the Internet will eventually cease to exist, and will have to for reasons outlined below.

The relationship between these various types of networks can be described graphically as follows:

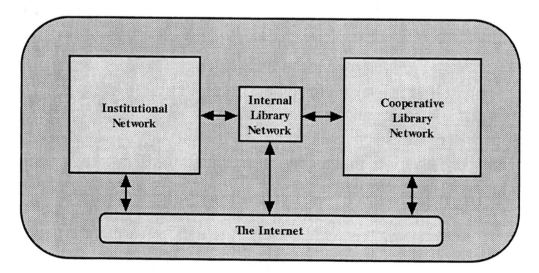

Figure 1: Types of networks

2.2 Electronic information resources

Networks form a mechanism through which users can access bibliographic resources and library services (e.g. by sending a request to the lending sub-system). This certainly enhances the process of finding and obtaining traditional, printed library materials. However, it is in the area of electronic information resources that the value of networks really comes into its own. This is because for electronic documents the network also gives access to the information content.

It is useful in the context of networks to make a distinction between various types of electronic information resources:

- Bibliographic resources, e.g. catalogues and other reference databases which describe available resources (both printed and electronic) and provide pointers to their location.

- Collections of full-text electronic documents (either created electronically or digitised from printed sources), made available on a stand-alone system or through document servers on a local network (e.g. within the library, the institution or a library specific network). These include locally produced materials and published materials distributed to libraries in electronic form.

- Off-line information products such as CD-ROM and CD-I (either stand-alone or connected to the local network).

- Traditional on-line resources, e.g. databases accessible through host organisations.

- Electronic resources available on the Internet (commonly indicated as *Networked Information Resources* or *NIRs*). Although access to most NIRs is currently uncontrolled and free of access, controlled access (e.g. through user registration and passwords) and fee-based access (based on networked payment mechanisms) are options which allow the addition of commercial and copyrighted materials to the range of networked information resources.

It should be noted that once libraries and library specific networks are connected to the global information infrastructure (i.e. the Internet), their electronic resources (OPACs, databases, document servers, networked CD-ROMs) become *networked* information resources in the sense described above. Here again, the distinction between library resources and Internet resources is disappearing from the user's viewpoint. In fact, one can expect that within the next few years the Internet will become the predominant channel for access to all electronic information resources (including the 'traditional' on-line databases offered by host organisations).

Current developments suggest that there is a potentially important role for libraries in providing *controlled* access to networked information resources. This role is modelled on the traditional role of the library as an intermediary between (commercial) publishers and end-users. Whenever access to information resources has to be controlled for financial and/or copyright reasons, access control can be licensed by the information provider to the library. The library then pays for the resource (as it does for other library materials such as books and journals) and makes sure that any use of the resources is restricted to what is allowable under the terms of the license and/or copyright regulations. This relieves the information provider of having to maintain a contractual and financial relationship with each and every user of the information resource[2].

The mix of resource types described above leads to a number of choices (to be addressed at a later stage in the project) for libraries, e.g.:

- The choice between different media options for the same resource (e.g. between a printed version, a CD-ROM or an on-line database).

- The choice of access method for end-users (e.g. in the library, through a library network or via the Internet).

Another issue of future significance to libraries is the evolving nature of electronic documents. Printed documents are typically distinct entities of a static, unchanging nature. Initially, electronic documents were just imitations of printed documents in electronic form. However, electronic documents are increasingly becoming *compound* and *dynamic* (Cleveland, 1995). *Compound* means that a document can consist of various distributed 'information objects', i.e. a document can consist of a number of sections, each of which can be at a different physical location. In addition, a document can include information metadata (e.g. author, revision history, status etc.), process information (how to obtain it, access rights, relationship to other documents or to steps in a work process), and links to external elements (such as datasets, graphics, images, fonts etc.). The electronic record of a document in a database system may consist of nothing else than pointers to these different elements. *Dynamic* means that any

---

[2]   This issue is described in more detail in section 0.

component of a document may change at any time, and that a document (or document-component) may exist only temporarily. It is clear that systems based on the notion that a document is a single physical entity that will not change and will remain in existence as long as it is held by the library, are not capable of handling this type of document.

From an initial analysis of the literature we conclude that more and more information is becoming available in electronic form, that the concept of an electronic document is becoming much more complex, and that these electronic resources are becoming *networked* information resources in the sense that they are becoming available, in one way or the other, through the Internet.

2.3 Libraries and the Internet

The relationship between the library world and the Internet is therefore the main scope of the Knowledge Models study. This is a deliberate choice, based on the conviction that the essence of knowledge mediation in the context of networked resources lies in providing access to all electronic resources world-wide which are accessible through the network infrastructure. Since the Internet is the *de facto* 'global' network infrastructure, libraries will have to expand their notion of networks from the specifically *library oriented* networks to the Internet.

The choice for emphasis on the Internet rather than on library specific networks is also motivated by concern for the future role of libraries. If it is not already the case that for library *users* 'the network' is the Internet rather than a library network, it will most certainly be so in a few years time. And since many users are beginning to regard the network as a primary source of information, there is a danger that libraries will lose their role as knowledge mediators for large groups of information users. In addition, information providers (e.g. publishers) are looking to the Internet as a channel for distributing their products. If libraries do not take on a role as 'controlled access providers', information providers will have to seek other ways of organising controlled access.

The only way to preserve the knowledge mediating role of libraries in the networked environment is to establish a firm relationship between libraries (including library networks) and the global network infrastructure. This can be done by linking the information world of libraries and the information world of the Internet.

Such a link can be interpreted in two different ways:

- Libraries will have to expand the range of knowledge resources to which they provide access to include electronic resources on the global network. In doing so, they will have to provide added value to end-users, based on their traditional functions in areas of collection building and preservation, resource discovery and navigation (e.g. the use of catalogues, indexes, bibliographies), document delivery and user support.

- Libraries will have to provide distant access to their knowledge resources (both bibliographic information and information content) to users through the Internet. This means that libraries themselves will have to make sure that users regard them as an important networked information resource in their own right.

Both forms of linking between libraries and the Internet are now being established by libraries, as indicated above. These two issues, together with the integration of network functions with traditional library functions, therefore form the themes of this report.

3. Library functions

The knowledge mediating function of the library is performed through a number of specific tasks. These include:

- Acquisition: obtaining information resources in order to store and provide access to them. An additional objective of this activity is often the preservation of documents in the interest of cultural heritage.
- Cataloguing and indexing: making the collection accessible, i.e. helping users to locate documents on the basis of formal (bibliographic) and/or content descriptors.
- Reference: providing pointers to information resources not necessarily contained in the user's own library.
- User services: making the information resources available through on-site consultation, lending, and document delivery
- Support: giving the user guidance and assistance.

Both the changing role of libraries and new developments in information technology and networking will influence the way in which these functions will have to be implemented in future. In the following paragraphs, we list some of the more important issues in the context of networked library services for each of the above-mentioned functions.

3.1 Acquisition

Support functions for acquisitions (including order record creation, status reports and claiming, checking-in of documents and handling of invoices) are nowadays common features of modern integrated library systems. The impact of networking in the field of acquisitions is expected to be found in two distinct areas:

- The link between libraries and suppliers (e.g. publishers, booksellers and subscription agents) within the administrative process (ordering, checking, claiming, invoicing). In this area, a number of proprietary solutions have been available for a number of years, usually offered by international journal agents. For a more open, generic solution, EDI (Electronic Data Interchange) technologies have some interesting advantages. In the UK, the Aston University library is investigating the implication of EDI technologies for the acquisition process.

- Electronic document delivery from supplier (e.g. publisher) to library. The traditional, printed form in which publications are delivered to the library, is increasingly perceived as having significant disadvantages. These include cost, lack of speed and inflexibility in the packaging of information. All parties involved, including publishers, libraries and end-users, could benefit from electronic, networked distribution. This would not only provide fast and cheap delivery, but would also allow much more selective acquisition, e.g. at the level of individual articles instead of entire journal titles. In addition, libraries increasingly need to have documents available in electronic form in order to distribute them to end-users or intermediary libraries, in the form of a copy, fax or over the network.

Especially in academic and special libraries, the emphasis in acquisitions has shifted from monographs to journals. It is not surprising, therefore, that many projects in the area of acquisitions focus on electronic distribution of journals and journal articles. While technical solutions for this are being developed, another issue is also becoming important. In many libraries, the traditional 'just in case' type of acquisition is changing into an approach based on 'just in time' availability. This implies a combination of acquisition of resources in direct response to users' requests, and refraining from acquisition in favour of resource sharing, i.e. using another library's resources instead of acquiring the document for the user's own library. In both cases the library depends on a system based on the following characteristics:

- A user-accessible, up-to-date overview of resources available directly from publishers or from other libraries, preferably based on enhanced content information.
- A system for fast delivery of documents from available source to end-user.
- Administrative and technical mechanisms for access control, copyright protection, invoicing, etc.

It is clear that this approach can only work if it is based on advanced catalogue and database systems, electronic information and digital networks.

The concept of acquisition is therefore changing as publications gradually become available in electronic form and can be distributed via electronic networks. The information made available by the library can be acquired more selectively, and be related more to specific user needs than used to be the case. Electronic interaction between end-users and libraries, in combination with the type of system described above, will make it possible to offer 'just in time' services efficiently. Ultimately, this will also have an impact on publishers and on the availability of information in the marketplace. This can be the case if libraries provide feedback on users' information needs and information use to publishers, or if publishers allow for direct interaction with end-users. Such feedback information will help publishers to tailor their products to specific user needs, to anticipate developments in user behaviour and to enhance the efficiency of the publishing process.

The spectacular growth of the Internet and the increase of networked information resources available through it, has special implications for the acquisitions function of libraries. These include the following:

- Libraries can provide pointers or 'road signs' (e.g. through Gopher menus and WWW home-pages) to network resources which are thought to be of interest to its users. This can be done using the same criteria as applied to the selection of resources in the traditional acquisitions function. It is interesting to note that in this case the distinction between acquisitions and referencing becomes blurred: providing a reference to a network resource makes it, from the user's viewpoint, as accessible as if it had been acquired by the library as part of its own collection.

- Libraries can also choose to acquire network resources as part of their own collection of (electronic) documents. Reasons for doing so might include improved speed of delivery, conversion to standard formats, enhanced cataloguing and (full-text) indexing, and guaranteeing availability over a longer period of time. It must be noted, however, that the evolving nature of compound, dynamic documents and more specifically the type of distributed hypertext documents one increasingly finds on the network (e.g. through WWW-servers) makes it extremely difficult to download this type of document from one system to another.

- Many libraries, especially within academic institutions and public organisations, will increasingly acquire documents in electronic manuscript form directly from authors in the parent institution, in order to make them available via the network. In other words, this type of acquisition could form the basis of an institutional publishing role for the library. This will require a new approach to the acquisitions function, involving the development of selection criteria for acquisition and publishing, developing an editorial function, etc.

3.2 Cataloguing, indexing and reference services

Traditionally, libraries provide descriptive cataloguing and subject indexing for monographs and journal titles through the catalogue. In general, cataloguing and indexing is not done for journal *contents* (i.e. individual articles). Cataloguing and indexing of journal articles is available through printed bibliographies and, increasingly, through on-line bibliographic databases. Therefore, the (on-line) catalogue, bibliographies and bibliographic databases are the three components of the 'window' through which the library provides access to knowledge sources to clients. Catalogues typically describe the 'holdings' or collection of a library or, in the case of 'central' or union catalogues, to a specified group of libraries. Bibliographies and on-line databases typically are independent of any specific physical collection and describe the body of literature published in a given field or geographic area.

In many cases items are not catalogued by each individual library but by a central cataloguing organisation or national library. Records for individual publications are obtained from these central organisations, after which local holdings information, subject identifiers, etc. are added.

Library catalogues provide direct access to publications by pointing to their physical location within the library. Bibliographies and on-line databases provide only indirect access. After identifying an item, the user has to check its availability in the library through the catalogue, or locate it in another library through a union catalogue or the library's interlibrary loan system.

This situation applies not only to printed publications, but equally to audio-visual materials and non-networked electronic publications on 'physical' media such as CD-ROM and CD-I. With networked information resources, however, the situation tends to be more complex.

Roughly, one can say that there are four ways for the library to help users to identify and obtain networked information resources:

1. Libraries catalogue and classify local resources and make them accessible through local OPACs. Increasingly these OPACs include descriptions of electronic items held by the library. The description of resources which already have been catalogued, in union catalogues, can be used by librarians for their own catalogue.

Libraries can include descriptions of network resources in the catalogue, preferably with a link (via a URL) to its electronic source on a networked document server. In order to guarantee availability, this will usually only be done for documents available on servers under the control of the library.

Items catalogued locally will find their way into on-line union catalogues, or national catalogues (NLS, BL, etc.) or bibliographic databases (e.g. WCLC, BLCMP, CURL).

At least two things are required:

- A means of enhancing catalogue records so that they can include the information needed to allow the electronic item to be retrieved from a remote networked source; in several countries existing cataloguing rules and formats have been adapted for this purpose.

- Client software capable of utilising this information to retrieve the item from the wide range of servers on the network and of displaying/playing the item once it has been retrieved; such software would preferably be integrated in the existing OPAC-system.

2. Libraries can also make available a comprehensive selection of the many existing directories of Gophers, FTP-sites, WWW-sites etc. This can either be done by retaining such lists within the library (e.g. in electronic form), or by providing pointers to their locations on the network. It is of course necessary to continuously update (the pointers to) these lists, in view of their dynamic nature.

An extensive effort is carried out by many individuals and organisations to impose some kind of structure onto the collection of resources constituted by the Internet. Examples of these are various directories of networked resources, Gopher menu structures (e.g. of the Clearinghouse for subject oriented Internet resources at University of Minnesota) and WWW index pages. These are often directed towards subject areas, document types or user groups. As may be expected, there even exist directories of directories in this area.

There exist several projects aimed at developing a uniform networked catalogue of the Internet, based on traditional library cataloguing concepts and standards. However, this is believed by many to be impractical, due to the sheer size and dynamic nature of the network. It is unlikely that a comprehensive, up-to-date catalogue can be maintained at an acceptable cost.

3. By maintaining a Gopher or WWW-site (managed by the library) which acts as an 'entry point' to the Internet by structuring available sources and providing links to other Gophers, WWW-sites and specific documents on the network.

4. By providing access to the various search tools now being implemented on the Internet. These tools automatically index large sections of the network and allow searches to be carried out using keywords and other identifiers. Examples of a subject catalogues on the Internet are the WWW VirtualLlibrary (maintained by CERN), ALIWEB and Yahoo.

In addition to enhancements to the OPAC for accessing documents located on the network, the library will also have to provide additional access tools, including Gopher and FTP clients, and WWW-browsers. These too, would preferably be integrated in or callable from the OPAC. An alternative approach is to use a WWW-browser as the end-user interface to all networked library functions, including the catalogue. Current browsers integrate WWW, Gopher, FTP, Telnet and E-mail client functions. A further step is to provide a WWW interface to the library catalogue using Z39.50 and the HTML Forms function[3].

Theise (1994) argues that URLs can be used to catalogue on-line resources in a way that will not conflict with emerging standards. He gives a description of the way how Internet resources (FTP, TELNET, MAIL/SMTP, Gopher, finger, HTTP, NEWS/NNTP, Prospero, WAIS/Z39.50 documents) can be catalogued.

Several interesting initiatives for cataloguing network resources have been undertaken:

• OCLC Internet resources cataloguing experiment: a working group of OCLC and the Library of Congress considers how librarians can create cataloguing records for on-line information resources. Guidelines have been written, and changes to

---

[3]   An example of an approach which integrates the OPAC with network tools is the networked catalogue of the University Library at Utrecht in the Netherlands. This catalogue can be accessed using standard WWW-browsers and includes hypertext links between data elements. The URL is: [http://pablo.bru.ruu.nl]. An overview of Z39.50-based library catalogues on the Internet which are accessible with standard WWW-browsers is available at:
[http://www.lib.ncsu.edu/staff/morgan/alcuin/wwwed-catalogs.html].
        Other links to Z39.50-based catalogues and databases are available at:
[http://vinca.cnidr.org/reference/reference.html].

USMARC format have been approved, including an identification of file type and a field for location and access (very much like a URL).

- Within the CATRIONA project several cataloguing activities have been undertaken (Nicholson, 1994a/b):

  - Local cataloguing of local electronic resources and of Internet resources of significance to the local situation.
  - Enhancement of the records (based on the MARC standard) so that they can include identifiers such as URLs and URNs.
  - Enhancement of a range of standard OPAC clients to give them web-type abilities to locate and retrieve electronic documents and WAIS type distributed search facilities.
  - Utilisation of distributed searching and co-operative cataloguing into larger central databases as the mechanism for enabling significant Internet resources to be found and retrieved by the user.
  - Questions of control and levels of access to different categories of local users have been considered.

- Within the ELDORADOC project of the University of Groningen (RUG) electronic documents are treated in the same way as printed documents. They are catalogued via the OPC (On-line Public Catalogue). The electronic sources can be accessed via the OBN (open Library network) and the Central Pica Catalogue, which are on Internet. Users can send documents via e-mail to his or her address. There also is a function to print the document on request. A number of problems encountered in the project are:

  - How to arrange the payment for the document delivery.
  - Acceptable viewers for MS Windows & UNIX Platforms were not readily available (viewer software requires specific hardware, for instance more than 8 MB internal memory and large hard disks).
  - A lack of PostScript printers .
  - Network bandwidth and pc-capacity, especially for users working at home.
  - Documents were expected to be made available in PostScript format or PDF (Portable Document Format ACROBAT/ADOBE), but it turned out that most were written in WordPerfect. Conversion proved to be difficult.
  - Documents have to be free of copyright for legal reasons, since there is no restriction on access.

- A co-operative approach to classification and description of network resources is being taken by the BUBL Information Service and NISS in the UK. A team of volunteers with specific subject interests identify and, in some cases, describe resources in their subject area. A template for the descriptions has been developed based on UDC (Universal Decimal Classification) to classify resources by subject.

The project InfoServices in the Netherlands is a joint initiative of the Royal Library (KB) and Surfnet. Here, the staff originally started to catalogue files on the server along library lines, but it was soon realised that this was not sustainable, and data providers were asked to provide a description of the resources with any submitted files. (Only material judged of interest or of durable value by staff is actually mounted). This description is stored alongside the file on the server where it can be inspected by the user. It was also decided to integrate these descriptions into the PICA database. The project developed a format for on-line resources based on the MARBI proposals[4], and PICA has implemented a format for on-line resources along these lines.

- The Heriot-Watt University Library in Edinburgh, together with a number of other libraries, will start the Edinburgh Engineering Virtual Library (EEVL) in August 1995[5]. This is a two-year project to build a gateway for the higher education and research community to facilitate access to high quality information resources in the field of engineering. When operational, users will be able to browse through and search for entries in the EEVL database of engineering resources, and dynamically connect to resources of interest. The EEVL gateway will be a WWW-interface. It will provide a central access point to networked information, mainly based on UK resources. Funding for the project is provided under the Access to Networked resources Programme Area of the Electronic Libraries Programme managed by the Joint Information Systems Committee (JISC) on behalf of the UK Higher Education Funding Councils.

Dempsey (1994a) gives a global description of the initiatives of libraries in the field of bibliographic metadata. He notes that libraries have invested heavily in the creation of catalogue records (local and union catalogues), and in many European countries there is a consolidated resource, in which the national monograph holdings, or some significant portion of them, are represented. These services allow the user to 'discover'

---

[4]   Cf. Library of Congress Network Development and Standards Office (1995).
[5]   Cf. [http://www.hw.ac.uk/libWWW/eevl/eevlhome.html].

resources, and in some cases to request their delivery. They often contain locators in the form of library holdings data. Libraries also provide access to abstracting and indexing services. Recently there has been a move towards (unmediated) end-user services, either on CD-ROM or by funding access to on-line resources (e.g. databases) for use within defined communities of users. However, usually these resources are subject-oriented: they do not represent a particular collection and they are not associated with holdings or location data.

The entire set of globally available bibliographic records is fragmented and divided over many different types of sources. Many of these, library OPACs primarily, are freely available on Internet, but others, such as union catalogues, national library resources, and abstracting and indexing services, are only available to certain closed user communities (e.g. registered library users or members of a library specific network). It is not possible to search more than one at the same time.

3.3 Consultation, lending and document delivery

With traditional printed documents, items can be consulted on-site, given on loan for a limited period of time, or provided in the form of a photocopy. New forms of document delivery are now being developed, which allow fax-based or electronic exchange of documents between libraries (for interlibrary lending purposes), and for delivery of documents by fax or e-mail to end-users outside the library.

Any service to users which implies duplication (either photocopying or electro-copying, especially if this implies creating a database of digitised publications) is subject to copyright regulations. Current developments in copyright law tend to be increasingly restrictive, especially with regard to digitising and electronic distribution in the context of document delivery.

In the case of networked information resources, two distinct cases have to be distinguished:

- Public domain materials. At present, the large majority of network resources is offered in the public domain, i.e. can be accessed freely by anyone wishing to do so. Although copyright applies to such documents, no copyright fees are expected to be paid. In this case, there are no restrictions on the access a library provides to these materials, and to personal use made of them by the users of the library.

- Commercial materials. Increasingly, the network is being used as a distribution medium for commercial publications, i.e. documents for which copyright fees have to be paid to the copyright holder (usually the publisher). Publishers can handle this in several ways, e.g.:

  - By requiring that copyright fees be paid prior to access, e.g. by means of a credit card or in future through 'electronic cash'.

  - By offering a license agreement to the library which stipulates the exact nature of the allowable use and the conditions under which the library is allowed to offer users access to the materials.

Although providing a copy of a network resource to a library user is not difficult in technical terms, major problems can therefore arise with commercial, copyright materials. libraries will have to take special measures to ensure that copyright fees are paid, and that fair use is made of documents provided to users.

There are two locations in which the interaction between a user and the library can take place: in the library itself or at the user's location ('at the user's desktop'). This leads in practice to the following three situations:

- User searches for and accesses a network resource in the library
- User searches for a network resource in the library and accesses it at his desktop
- User searches for network resource from his own location (using the library as a network access point) and accesses it at the desktop

In the latter situation, the library becomes merely one of the many access points on the network.

These three situations are described in the following matrix:

Search	Consult	
	In the library	*At user's desktop*
In the library	- Access library search mechanism (OPAC, Gopher, WWW) in the library - View item in the library (e.g. via browser/viewer)	- Access library search mechanism (OPAC, Gopher, WWW) in the library - Transfer resource to user's desktop (e.g. via e-mail)
At user's desktop		- Access library search mechanism (OPAC, Gopher, WWW) through the network - Transfer resource to user's desktop (e.g. via browser, FTP or E-mail)

Figure 2: Access methods

Certain technical provisions are necessary in order to support the functionality described in the matrix:

- Networked information resources exist in a wide variety of formats, and tend to be increasingly multimedia. For on-site consultation of network resources, the library has to make available a comprehensive array of so-called document viewers capable of presenting (and if possible printing) any type of document. This will include viewers for various document types (e.g. word processor formats, SGML, Postscript, Adobe) and media types (e.g. text, images, video and sound).

- In many cases a user who identifies a network resource through the library will wish to receive it at his or her own desktop location, either directly through downloading (file transfer) or via electronic mail. This is usually not a problem if the user access the sources - via the library - from his or her desktop. If access takes place at the physical library location, the library will have to provide facilities for transferring the document to the user's pc or network location. If necessary, the library will also have to provide any viewers necessary for accessing the document.

3.4 User support

Libraries are not merely places where users come to find documents and to consult them or take them away on loan or as a photocopy. Libraries also provide a wide range of support to their users. Important areas of support are:

- Training in the use of library systems and resources.
- Guidance in formulating searches for finding information on specific subjects, questions and problems.
- Support in using resource finding systems such as catalogues, bibliographies, on-line databases, CD-ROM's and special types of media (e.g. audio-visual media).
- Administrative support, e.g. for interlibrary lending and document delivery.

In the area of networked information resources, a number of new support tasks can be identified. These include:

- Technical support for using network tools (e.g. browsers, viewers).
- Guidance in choosing and navigating specific resource spaces.
- Qualitative guidance with respect to selecting relevant and useful resources.
- Support for using new types of media (e.g. hypertext and multimedia).
- Guidance for managing private collections of network information resources at the user's desktop.
- Support in the area of network communication and publishing.

It should be noted that network related support need not be confined to the use of tools and resources within the library. Many users who access networked resources at their desktop without even using the library as such, encounter numerous problems in using network tools and finding their way through resource spaces. Libraries can offer support in these areas which often cannot easily be obtained elsewhere. Libraries can provide added value with this type of support to the extent that they are able to relate support actions to the specific characteristics and requirements of these users.

Since users will increasingly access library functions from a distance (e.g. from home or from their workplace), distance access to library support functions will be necessary as well.

3.5 Digital libraries?

Developments in networking offer opportunities to libraries for providing new modes of access to users in two distinct areas:

- distance access to the library's knowledge resources and user support
- access through the library to networked information resources

It is often said that libraries will in future become 'digital libraries'. The assumptions which underlie this belief has recently been questioned by Levy and Marshall (1995). They maintain that libraries will have to offer integrated access to both printed and electronic materials for a long period of time. Their analysis is interesting and can be summarised as follows:

- The traditional view of libraries is that they provide access to documents which remain relevant for a long period of time and which do not change or change only slowly. In future, libraries will also have to provide access to documents which are highly dynamic (i.e. change frequently and exist in many variations) and to documents which have a very short lifetime (i.e. need only to be retained for a short period of time). Libraries will have to develop methods for coping with these characteristics.

- Even before the network era, libraries have contained materials based on a variety of 'technologies': printed documents, manuscripts, audio-visual materials and off-line electronic products (e.g. CD-ROM's). Networked resources are but an addition to this range of materials. It is inconceivable that the current holdings of libraries can be transformed to electronic, networked form in the short term. A narrow focus on digital technologies is insufficient, and the concept of 'digital' libraries is misleading.

- A final assumption questioned by Levy and Marshall is that libraries are used by individuals working alone. In practice, collaborative work is the predominant pattern. Therefore, libraries will have to develop support for communication and collaboration between users accessing the library's knowledge resources.

3.6 Libraries in the networked environment

Developments in the field of information technology and networking have consequences for libraries on several levels: for the individual library, for the relations between libraries, and for the relations between libraries and the rest of the world. In this section we shall examine these three levels.

3.6.1 Networking for the individual library

Developments in information technology and networking have been used by libraries in order to modernise their services. However, the development of telematics on the basis of electronic networks is leading to new challenges.

Increasing role of electronic information in the library.

A large proportion of libraries in Europe now use automated catalogues and hold their bibliographic records in electronic form. Many of these libraries are connected to networks, either locally (e.g. campus networks) or through gateways to the Internet. Information resources themselves, as held in or obtainable through the library, are increasingly available in electronic form. In addition, the administrative housekeeping functions of the library are in many cases automated as well. All this means that libraries are as familiar with electronic information as any other modern organisation.

Libraries are now starting to digitise parts of their paper collections and convert them to machine-readable formats. This is not only done locally, but also within a number of large-scale projects. For example, the G7 members together with the European Commission have identified a number of projects, to be based on international co-operation, which aim at demonstrating the potential of the information society. One of these projects is the Electronic Libraries Project which has as its objective: to constitute from existing programs including digital collections a large distributed virtual collection of the humankind knowledge available to a large public via networks. The project is expected to improve availability at international level of digitised resources including both the bibliographic records and the information content itself, integrating text, graphics, still images, sound and video. It will promote the large scale digitisation of material on electronic library systems[6]. In the United States the Library of Congress has announced an ambitious effort to convert into digital form the most important materials in its collection and in the collection of all public and research

---

[6] Further information is available from the Commission's WWW-server at [http://www.echo.lu].

libraries in the United States. Conversions are undertaken for preservation and space reasons and above all for better and easier access by users.

A great benefit of electronic resources is that they can be used by multiple users from multiple locations. Libraries will need to provide their users with appropriate access and manipulation tools for using the electronic resources. In the long run, this will necessitate a move towards networking in order to access information resources on the global network, to provide access to the library's catalogues and reference tools from the user's workplace, and to transfer documents from the library to the user.

Future requirements for libraries in this area are:

- Increased acquisition of electronic publications (e.g. on CD-ROM or CD-I)
- Increased access to networked information resources
- Digitisation and networking of existing printed resources
- Distant access to all user-oriented functions of the library

Library systems

Many libraries have installed integrated systems in order to automate the various library processes: acquisitions, cataloguing and indexing, lending and document delivery, as well as management functions. In the area of acquisitions EDI-technology is beginning to be used.

In general, the systems currently installed in libraries are suitable for the traditional library tasks and processes. But due to a lack of 'openness' it is often difficult to incorporate new developments into these systems. This is particularly true for network related functions which require that a system can be easily adapted and can be linked to different types of systems. A basic problem of many library systems is therefore that they tend to become isolated, and to lag behind in developments. This is a problem not only because libraries cannot offer the advanced services which users are becoming to expect. It also prevents libraries from presenting themselves in a professional and convincing way to their clients. Any comparison of the highly graphical network tools with the traditional character-based user interfaces of most library systems will demonstrate the point.

Document delivery is not commonly a functional component of the library system. Requests for documents usually have to be written down on printed request forms, or passed on to the library by phone or facsimile. Document delivery is handled via mail or fax. This leads to a paradoxical situation: with help of OPACs and other tools the discovery of resources can be done very fast, but actually obtaining the resource is often very slow. Resource discovery and resource delivery are not integrated. What users expect, however, in a networked environment is integration of precisely these two functions.

Future requirements for libraries in this area are:

- Open library systems, based on official or de facto standards, which can easily accommodate new functions developed by third parties, and which can be interlinked with other systems.

- User-friendly, graphical interfaces which are accessible through the network and offer a level of ease and attractiveness comparable to that of other network tools.

- Integrated functionality, especially combining resource discovery and document delivery.

Management of library services in an electronic environment

In general, existing management tools and management systems have been developed to support traditional library operations and services based on paper collections. However, the inclusion of new electronic materials in library collections will require appropriate new administrative tools. Also, there is a need to reconsider the traditional work flows in libraries and the way libraries interact with their users, with other departments and services in their organisation and with their suppliers (Text of Telematics/Libraries Programme CfP, 1995).

According to Zhao (1994) the management of an electronic library involves five areas of activity: management of data, management of users, usage statistics management, printing management and management of software and hardware. Much work still has to be carried out in these areas.

Future requirements of libraries for managing electronic materials are:

- Tools for management of electronic documents held within the library.
- Tools for managing the use of information and systems resources by users.

- Tools for planning and monitoring work processes in the 'electronic' library.
- Tools for managing access and copyright issues.

3.6.2 Networking between libraries and interconnected library services

Co-operation in the area of library services

Libraries already have a history of co-operation and resource sharing, mainly through interlending systems and organisational frameworks for shared cataloguing. Information technology and networking offer even more opportunities for co-operation and interconnections between libraries. This leads to the concept of 'interconnected services' in which the services of a group of interconnected libraries are offered to the user as a single enhanced service. This concept presupposes integration and interconnection at the functional level: a catalogue search would have to be carried out in all interconnected catalogues at the same time; a request for document delivery would have to be serviced by any library holding the document.

At the present moment, there is insufficient integration between the various services and functions to allow for interconnected library services to end-users. One of the main reasons for this is a lack of standardisation or, in some cases, use of existing standards, at a number of levels: open library systems, user and systems interfaces, standards for search, access, and retrieval of library materials.

Bibliographic data creation and sharing between libraries

An area where co-operation between libraries has been successful in many countries is that of shared cataloguing. To quote Dempsey (1994a): 'A complex apparatus exists for the creation and sharing of records, and in many European countries there is a consolidated resource, in which the national monograph holdings, or some significant portion of them, are represented. In the form of OCLC, there is also a significant international resource which contains approaching 30 million individual titles reflecting in very many more holdings. Other large reservoirs also exist.' As can be imagined, the utilisation of such reservoirs is greatly enhanced by networks capable of providing easy access anywhere in the world. In this way, bibliographic resources can become available on a cost-per-item basis to libraries not explicitly participating in a co-operative network.

It remains to be seen to what extent the concept of a local library catalogue will remain valid in the networked environment. For networked resources as such, catalogues are to a certain extent being replaced by indexes and search mechanisms which are integrated into the network itself. These act effectively as end-user accessible union catalogues which describe resources available from vast number of document collections on the Internet. These mechanisms integrate, of course, resource discovery and document delivery. It is not difficult to imagine that in future, local cataloguing could consist of adding to a shared bibliographic data resource (located on the network) a pointer to local holdings. This pointer would, when accessed by the user, either lead to document delivery over the network, or to a loan or delivery request to be satisfied via mail or fax.

3.6.3 Library access to networked information resources

The amount of resources and services available via Internet is increasing steadily. These resources are made available by individuals, institutions in the academic world and the public sector, publishers and other commercial organisations, and also by libraries themselves. With this increasing amount of resources it becomes very difficult for a user to find out which resources and services are available and how they can be accessed. Methods for resource description are needed in order to find and retrieve the information one wants. Tools which facilitate resource discovery, access and retrieval need to be improved. The role of libraries as an intermediary for finding and using resources is influenced by these developments.

Libraries as providers of networked information resources

Libraries, among others, use the Internet as a medium to publish their information resources. Most electronic information services provided by libraries are in fact collections of metadata (local and shared catalogues, abstracting and indexing services). Already many hundreds of OPACs are available on the Internet. However, they are poorly integrated with other network resources and with access, discovery and retrieval tools. Access is by remote login (Telnet); a move to client-server systems based on the SR and Z39.50 protocols has only just begun.

These library resources are based on a large variety of library systems, which means that users are confronted with a highly heterogeneous resource space. In contrast with the World Wide Web, for instance, which provides a uniform interface to all resources on the Web, many different user interfaces (OPACs) have to be used in order to access a number of different catalogues, there is no integration or linking. The bibliographic record is fragmented and resides in many databases of varying scope. Some are freely available on Internet, others are only available to certain closed user communities. There is of course a need for integration, but for the moment integration is reached by consolidation of data (e.g. through union catalogues), not by access, distributed searching or navigation.

Libraries also act as publishers of information resources on the Internet. These resources are often digitised paper resources; the National Digital Library project of the Library of Congress is an example of a project where digitisation is undertaken on a large scale in order to provide networked access to traditional library resources. Another area where libraries are involved as network publishers is concerned with making (digital) materials of the parent organisation (e.g. a university) available on the network. These resources include dissertations, research materials, datasets etc.

A further way for libraries to create a presence on the network is to set up a 'home page' on the World Wide Web. Through this mechanism, libraries can provide information on library services, opening times, rules etc. They can also provide links to support services (e.g. help files), the OPAC (either via Telnet or through a Z39.50 interface) local file servers, and document delivery services[7].

Libraries as intermediaries for finding and using resources

Tools and standards for resource description, access and retrieval are required in order to find and use resources. At this moment many tools are available, but there is not yet a widely used standard for resource description, nor are there sufficiently standard methods for resource classification and indexing. As mentioned above, the current Internet tools for resource discovery, access and retrieval are not well integrated with library systems with the same functionality. Although OPACs are in many cases accessible via the network, the user becomes isolated from other library services (lending, support) and other network resources, services and tools once connected to the library catalogue. On the other hand, libraries can (and do) provide access to the network within the library, but this is no different from accessing the network from another location, e.g. the user's workplace. This lack of integration leads to a conspicuous lack of added value from the library.

---

[7]   Many of the numerous resource listings on the World Wide Web also refer to library home pages. The Infofilter project in the United States offers critical reviews of a number of these pages and can be reached at [http://192.135.229.51/inteval.htm].

What is needed, therefore, is further integration of library functions and resources into the networked environment. A number of necessary steps are:

- Networked access to union catalogues and local library systems through standard network interfaces (which nowadays means WWW browsers)
- Integrated access to all library functions (resource discovery, e.g. catalogues, document servers, lending and document delivery, support)
- Facilities for downloading bibliographic descriptions and resources identifiers/locators
- Creation of hyperlinked bibliographic records
- Access to the network from library systems, e.g. OPACs
- Further digitisation of library resources
- Methods for indexing sets of library catalogues (e.g. within subject or geographic areas) and integration with existing networked indexing systems.

3.6.4 Problems and challenges

From this brief review of consequences of information technology and networking for libraries we can extract some of the more important problems and challenges for libraries as knowledge mediators in a networked environment.

Problems

- Lack of clear legislation for electronic copyright, which prevents libraries from developing document delivery services and offering resources over the network
- Lack of secure payment systems for using network resources;
- Problems in managing versions and assuring authenticity and integrity of electronic documents
- Lack of digital material other than meta-information (bibliographic records)
- Lack of stability and preservation of networked information resources, resulting in loss of long-term availability
- Lack of integration of services and resources from different libraries
- Lack of integration between Internet tools and systems, which are organised along client-server lines, and library applications, which are still characterised by terminal access to multiple isolated applications;
- Lack of contact between the library community and the Internet community; both at system level and at service level.

Challenges

- One of the main challenges for libraries will be to maintain a position as knowledge mediators in a world where users increasingly expect to be able to access information via networks. If libraries do not integrate with the networked environment, they will become isolated and their resources will become increasingly under-utilised. Libraries can provide added value by assisting users to cope with the increasing amount of resources which are available via Internet. Libraries can provide their experience and knowledge in the field of description and retrieval of resources, developing special collections, and user support in order to help human beings to deal with the information overload. Libraries are also in a position to develop archival and preservation functions for the network.

- There is no longer a need to interact with separate resource discovery systems. Whether a document is available on a file server in the user's local library, in another library or document supply centre, or somewhere on the network becomes unimportant. Integration between library systems and network resource discovery systems will be a major challenge in the next few years. This could be reached by gateways between library systems and network systems. It also requires integration of library access methods and metadata services in integrated information services, based upon publicly defined protocols and formats and resource identification (Dempsey, 1994a).

- The network infrastructure will not only consist of technical resource discovery systems (although this has currently the most attention). There will also be a need for resource discovery *services,* which integrate resource discovery systems and which offer services within a particular domain and add value specific to its purposes. (This need already has been recognised in the 'Info Services Project' by SURF and the Royal Library in the Netherlands.) The Library community has to realise that it can play an important role in the design and delivery of such services. The linking between such services and library resource discovery services will have to be given high priority.

- Library networking not only changes the function of libraries, it also changes the role of libraries in the information chain. Libraries have to reconsider their role in the information chain, together with other parties (including publishers and parent organisations, e.g. universities and government organisations). In particular there is a challenge for libraries to maintain a position as the primary gateway to commercially published information in the networked environment.

A special problem which is discussed in more detail in section 0, deserves to be mentioned here. That is the problem of language. The predominant language of resources available on the Internet is currently English. However, materials in other languages are now being added. In addition, top-level entry points to networked resources (e.g. Gopher main menus and WWW home pages) are often available in a number of languages (usually the local language and English). The problem of accessing and understanding information in a foreign language which the user does not master, is extremely difficult. In spite of major efforts in the area of machine-translation, practical and affordable solutions do not as yet exist. However, there is at least a need for a mechanism which allows users to select materials which are available in their own language, i.e. to exclude materials in other languages. Some private companies are now active in this area by developing network browsers which can handle foreign character sets and are capable of selecting materials in a certain language[8]. This is a major effort, since it involves the development of 'internationalised' browsers and language-sensitive search engines on the Internet.

---

[8]   One such example was presented by Alis technologies Inc. at the 3rd World Wide Web Concertation Meeting at Brussels, June 20, 1995. See also [http://alis.ca:8082/].

PART 2: CONCEPTUAL ANALYSIS

4. The basic functions of knowledge mediation

In this part of the study we develop a conceptual analysis of knowledge mediation, focusing on the mechanisms by which the library links users to knowledge resources. Our point of departure is the future library which provides integrated access to all available knowledge resources: print and electronic, locally held and available through electronic networks.

In our analysis, we identify the complexities of knowledge mediation in such an integrated and networked environment and the many options open to libraries and their users. We also point to certain types of solutions which can help to optimise end-user oriented knowledge mediation.

From a conceptual viewpoint the library as a knowledge mediator performs three basic functions in providing access to knowledge for their users. These three functions are (cf. Figure 3):

- Making available various types of knowledge resources.

- Providing resource discovery mechanisms which allow users to identify relevant or requested resources and their locations.

- Providing mechanisms for delivery of specific resources to the user; delivery includes both obtaining a resource when it is not already available

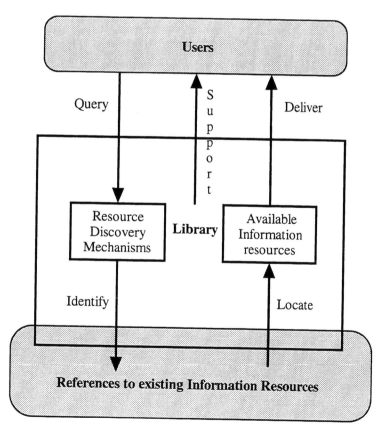

Figure 3: Knowledge mediation

in the library, and passing it on to the user in a suitable way.

These three functions involve decisions to be made both at the level of the library and at the level of the user:

- The library has to decide which knowledge resources, discovery mechanisms and delivery mechanisms are to be made available to its users; other decisions are relate to the way in which these functions are to be related or integrated and presented to the user.

- The user has to decide which discovery mechanisms, knowledge resources and delivery methods should be chosen for a specific information seeking task.

We regard these decisions as key issues in the knowledge mediation process. Libraries will have to make decisions in order to organise themselves for knowledge mediation, and they will have to support users in making appropriate decisions for carrying out the knowledge seeking process.

5. Acquiring information in the library

From the user's viewpoint, the library is a place where he or she can obtain items of information or knowledge resources. These knowledge resources, the sources of knowledge the user wishes to acquire, are either available in the library, obtainable through the library (e.g. from another library) or obtainable from the network.

In order to identify and locate specific knowledge resources, the library also provides a number of resource discovery mechanisms.

A resource discovery system contains some or all of the following components:

- document descriptions
- abstract and/or full text
- pointers to document locations(s)
- indexed search and/or sorted or hierarchical browse mechanism

Since libraries often offer a number of different discovery mechanisms the user has to choose between alternatives. This is done at two levels:

- choosing the discovery mechanisms *type* (e.g. library catalogue or network browser);

- choosing a specific discovery mechanism (e.g. Gopher or WWW).

Resource location

- provided by discovery mechanism (e.g. library catalogue, network browse or search mechanism)

- obtained through second search in location-providing discovery mechanism (usually library catalogue or journals list)

Resource provision

- from user's own library
- from other library (ILL/DocDel) or document provider
- from network

Resource delivery

- on-site consultation
- photocopy

Figure 4: Resource discovery

As discussed in more detail in section 0, the choice of discovery mechanism restricts the *resource space*, i.e. the set of resources that can be found using that mechanism.

In some cases the location of a document has to be assessed after the resource has been identified. This is usually done by looking up the resource in another discovery systems which does provide locations (e.g. a library (union) catalogue or journals list).

Once a resource has been identified and located, it has to be provided by the library, either from its own resources, from another library or document provider (via ILL or document Delivery) or from the global network. The final step is the actual delivery to the user by giving it for on-site consultation, making a photocopy, or sending it by mail, fax or e-mail. In the case of networked resources, these steps are often integrated, i.e. once a resource has been found (identified), it can immediately be accessed and, if necessary downloaded, printed or transferred to the user's location via e-mail.

The process of acquiring information is summarised in Figure 4.

In this process, three key issues are important to the user:

- Decisions to be made whenever alternative options are available at the various steps in the process of acquiring information.

- Issues related to the quality of information resources, i.e. how to ensure that information obtained through resource discovery is of sufficient quality and/or how to judge the quality of resources that are obtained.

- The issue of language, which is important in the context of a multilingual Europe and a global networked environment which is predominantly based on the English language.

These three issues will be discussed in subsequent sections of this report.

6. Organising the knowledge mediation function

The range of resource types and resource discovery mechanisms available to library users has expanded greatly due to the development of new electronic media and electronic networks. In the traditional library the available resources consist mainly of printed books and journals, while discovery mechanisms are restricted to catalogues and bibliographic reference works.

In the modern, networked library the range of options has increased dramatically. Printed resources contained in other libraries have become more easily available to users in their own library. New types of knowledge resources have become available, including:

- Microforms and audio-visual materials
- CD-ROM based and other electronic knowledge resources
- On-line databases of knowledge resources
- Electronic resources available on local document servers
- Networked knowledge resources (i.e. electronic resources available on the global network infrastructure, e.g. the Internet)

At the same time - and of necessity in order to access these new resources - new types of resource discovery mechanisms have become available, including:

- Shared (union) catalogues and access to other library catalogues
- Search interfaces for specific CD-ROM based and on-line bibliographic databases
- A range of network browsing mechanisms
- A range of network search mechanisms

All this means that the range of options for users and the number of choices to be made in finding information resources has increased significantly. In other words: the knowledge seeking process has become much more complex. Libraries have to find ways to help their users cope with this complexity and to help them make optimal use of the library's knowledge mediation function.

The broad range of resources created by the integration of electronic documents and networks complicates the task of organising and managing the library. The library not only has to handle more types of reference and knowledge resources, but also has to do this in such a way that its users can cope with the increased complexity. In other words, the library has to make certain decisions on resources, organise these resources by setting up appropriate technical and organisational infrastructures, and develop user support functions.

A general overview of the main decision areas and subsequent actions is presented in Figure 5.

Decisions	Actions
Types of resources within the library	• Decide on types of resources to be acquired by the library • Develop acquisition guidelines • Set up an infrastructure for acquiring, processing and making available resources
Types of resources from other sources	• Decide on types of resources to be obtained from other sources • Establish relationships with other organisations (e.g. for document delivery) where necessary
Discovery mechanisms	• Decide on types of discovery mechanisms to be made available • Develop strategies for integration and presentation of resource discovery methods (cf. section 0) • Set up an infrastructure for acquiring / creating and using discovery mechanisms
Provision methods	• Set up an infrastructure for obtaining resources from other sources
Transfer methods	• Decide on delivery methods to be made available • Develop guidelines for choice and use of delivery methods • Set up an infrastructure for resource transfer
User support	• Decide areas and steps in the knowledge mediation process where user support is required • Decide on support methods (e.g. face-to-face, manuals, on-line help) • Develop manuals, help-screens etc. • Set up procedures and infrastructure for user support
Bibliographic	• Establish guidelines for bibliographic description of

control	networked resources, including access data
	• Set up mechanisms for acquiring descriptive and access data from second sources if required
	• Set up procedures and infrastructure for cataloguing networked resources
Quality aspects	• Develop guidelines for assessing and maintaining the quality of networked resources
	• Set up quality control procedures
	• Set up procedures for pre-selection of high-quality resources

Figure 5: Knowledge mediation decisions

Perhaps the most important decision for libraries in the context of networked services is that between acquiring and storing knowledge resources in the library on the one hand, and providing access to knowledge resources on the other hand. This pertains to the more general choice between 'just in case' (acquisition) and 'just in time' (access), e.g. when the library has to choose between physically acquiring a publication and making it available through resource sharing with other libraries, using interlibrary lending and document delivery. In the context of networked knowledge resources, the decision is governed by factors such as:

• *Economics*: the cost of local storage versus network costs of access and the cost of maintaining reliable links to networked resources; especially for frequently used materials, local storage could be the cheapest option;

• *Availability*: local storage offers a better guarantee of continued availability than network access, since networked resources can be removed from their original location, and networks or document servers may frequently be congested or even unavailable;

• *Quality of resources*: the library could use acquisition and local storage as a way to pre-select resources and offer a 'restricted window' on materials of sufficient quality;

• *User access to networks*: if users (and perhaps the library itself) have limited access to external networks, i.e. if end-user access to networks is not feasible, then local storage of networked resources could be the only way to make these resources available to the user;

- *Ease of use*: local storage enhances the accessibility and speed of access for the user; resources can be stored in a more suitable format if necessary; resources can be integrated in available library systems which may provide additional features and greater ease of use than external network tools.

- *Resource management*: use of locally stored resources can be more easily monitored than access to external; sources; usage data provides management information on aspects such as type and volume of use of electronic resources.

Another way of describing the options for availability of knowledge resources is give in Figure 6:

	Non-networked knowledge resources (mostly in printed form)	Networked knowledge resources (in electronic form)
Pre-selected	Acquired and stored locally	Acquired and stored locally
		Accessible through the network based on pre-selection (e.g. using URL links in the catalogue, databases containing links to resources, Gopher menu's, WWW pages)
Not pre-selected	Resources acquired by other libraries: - Identifiable through printed form electronic bibliographies, other libraries' catalogues, national union catalogues, etc. - Obtainable through ILL, document delivery services, etc.	Other networked resources available through network tools

Figure 6: Options for knowledge resources

Here we see that in the context of networked resources - and from the user's viewpoint - the concept of 'pre-selection' is perhaps more useful than the concept of 'acquisition'. What is important to the user is that the library offers a coherent and well-structured set of resources (as a selective window to the body of knowledge) which can be identified and obtained in an easy way. Traditionally this set is created through acquisition and cataloguing of resources. In the networked library. this also includes the creation of links to pre-selected resources on the network. In other words, the library has to decide:

- which knowledge resources are to be acquired and stored locally;
- which resources are to be made accessible on a pre-selective basis;
- the extent to which other resources are to be made accessible in a general, non-selective way.

Other decisions that libraries have to make in organising for networked knowledge mediation pertain to the other issues described in this analysis, e.g. choice and integration of search mechanisms, provision and transfer of resources to the user, user support, bibliographic control, and quality issues.

7. Integrated resource discovery: strategies for reducing complexity

In the previous section we have described the expanding range of resources and discovery mechanisms which enhance knowledge mediation in the networked environment. We have also argued that this creates a level of complexity which can be difficult for users to cope with. Libraries have to develop strategies to reduce complexity in order to provide added value to their users.

The most fundamental problem created by the developments described above, is the availability of a large number of resource discovery mechanisms. The reason why this is so fundamental, is that for the user each discovery mechanism is an initial entry point to the 'knowledge space' where he or she expects to find relevant information. Making the right choice at the beginning of the search process has major implications for its success and for the effort involved in finding relevant resources, for the comprehensiveness of the results, for the quality of information received and for the speed of its delivery.

Different resource discovery mechanisms lead to different types of resources. For instance, the OPAC normally identifies only publications (usually not including journal articles) available in the library; bibliographies (printed, on CD-ROM or in on-line databases) identify a broader range of resources (especially journal articles) which may or may not be easily obtainable from the library; network discovery tools identify a specific sub-set of available resources (i.e. mainly public domain electronic documents), etc.

Having to choose a specific type of resource discovery mechanisms therefore limits the range of resources that can be found and/or forces the user to adopt a multiple information seeking strategy by performing the same search with a number of discovery mechanisms.

Furthermore, the choice of discovery mechanism also has consequences for the location and delivery functions. A resource listing from a bibliography has to be checked against the OPAC or journals list. Printed materials may have to be photocopied or obtained from another library, whereas networked electronic documents can be accessed directly.

A fundamental question is at which point the user should be forced to choose a certain resource type. Should this choice be related to the choice of resource discovery mechanisms, or should it be made after resources have been identified and located? End-users seem to desire ease of access and one-stop-shopping or, in other words, a minimum of a priori choices to be made and systems to be used.

Ideally, therefore, the library should provide a single resource discovery system for all existing resources within a specific domain covered by the library. In practice, this is not feasible. Printed discovery mechanisms (e.g. printed bibliographies) for which no electronic alternative exists cannot be included in an electronic system. In practice, it is not always easy to merge all available bibliographic databases (catalogues, on-line databases, CD-ROM's) into a single bibliographic system. The same applies to networked search and browse systems.

A number of strategies can be identified which could help libraries to optimise knowledge mediation for their users by reducing complexity in the available options. These include:

1. Creating a single access point to all resource discovery mechanisms available to the user;
2. Integrating bibliographic systems as far as possible in order to limit the number of alternative discovery mechanisms;
3. Creating mechanisms for automatically linking from resource discovery systems to electronic resources;
4. Creating mechanisms for mapping identifiers to locations where possible and appropriate;
5. Providing guidance to the user in choosing alternative systems and resources;
6. Organising knowledge mediation on a domain basis;
7. Use of intelligent agents;
8. Information filtering;
9. Workplace integration

We now discuss these strategies in more detail.

0.1   Single access point to resource discovery mechanisms

A single access point should be created which can be thought of as a map of the library's resources and resource discovery sub-systems. It should assist the user to make optimal use of the library by setting out a course for achieving a specific task, and guide the user to the most appropriate set of resources and/or resource discovery system(s) for that task.

0.2   Integration of bibliographic systems

Limiting the number of alternative resource discovery systems can be achieved by integrating as many resource types as possible in a single search system, e.g. the OPAC. Ideally, this system should include references to all resources with a specified location, e.g. monographs, journals (or possibly journal articles), subject specific resource discovery systems (e.g. CD-ROM's, important Gophers and WWW home pages, network resource lists etc.), electronic documents directly available on document servers, and URLs of important networked documents. These references should clearly describe the type of resource, and on-line help should be available in order to assist the user in choosing that type of resource.

0.3   Linking discovery systems and resources

For electronic resources, the main resource discovery mechanism should provide an automatic link to the appropriate access mechanism. For instance, a reference to a CD-ROM publication should provide the option to switch to that CD-ROM on a CD-ROM server; a reference to a networked document should call up the appropriate network access tool (e.g. an FTP, Gopher or WWW client) with the resource's URL. If this linking mechanism is not possible, on-line help should be available to assist the user in accessing the resource by other means. Ideally, such links to network tools should also be created for other resource discovery systems such as CD-ROMs if they describe networked resources.

A mechanism could also be created which identifies and automatically accesses resources found through network browsers which are available locally (i.e. stored on a local server).

0.4   Mapping bibliographic data to locations

Mechanisms are now being developed which map the output of a search on an electronic bibliographic database (e.g. on a CD-ROM) to locations found in the library's catalogue or journals list[9]. This will immediately identify the resources available locally and relieve the user from having to search each individual item in the

---

[9]   Research in this area is currently being carried out in the MECANO project under the European Commission's Libraries Programme.

---

library catalogue. This approach can also be applied to union catalogues and expanded to create automatic ILL or document delivery requests.

0.5 Assistance for user decisions

In general, whenever alternative search mechanisms, resources or locations are presented to the user, or when the user has to switch to a different discovery or access mechanism, the system should provide guidance to the user on how to proceed.

0.6 Organising knowledge mediation on a domain basis

In many cases the complexity of knowledge mediation can be reduced by creating a coherent set of discovery mechanisms, information resources, support functions etc. on a (subject) domain basis. For instance, in some areas few electronic or networked resources may be available and the preferred entry point would be the on-line catalogue. In other areas, especially where electronic publishing is predominant and timeliness is important, network tools are the preferred instrument for resource discovery. A number of domain based network gateway services are already being developed[10] which can serve as a 'one-stop-shopping' access point for networked resources in that domain. If developments in this area catch on, we shall see the emergence of domain based electronic libraries. An alternative strategy for libraries would then be to develop towards a 'top-level virtual library' providing access to a range of specialised domain based electronic libraries on a national, European or even global basis. Another alternative is to use domain based services as a convenient source for selecting resources in specific domains to be included in one's own library. This issue will be discussed in more detail in the third report (Application Models) of the Knowledge Models project.

0.7 Use of intelligent agents

Intelligent agents (also called 'web-crawlers') are software tools currently under development which search the global network in order to find resources. They select relevant resources based on criteria such as subject, currency and quality. They can be used to maintain a single catalogue for a specific domain, or for searching the entire resource space for an individual user. They can either be used as a comprehensive

---

[10] For instance, under the FIGIT Electronic Libraries Programme in the United Kingdom, gateways are being developed in various domains, including art, design and architecture, medicine, the social sciences and engineering. These are in effect 'virtual electronic libraries', providing a single access point to electronic resources in their respective domains.

---

search tool or for current awareness purposes (i.e. to identify new resources). This approach can relieve the user of the many complexities of resource discovery on the Internet. It should be noted, however, that these intelligent agents have not yet reached a full stage of development, and that problems of integration and of accessing retrieved links to resources remain.

0.8   Information filtering

Another way of reducing complexity for users is to develop information filtering services based on user profiles. The concept of information filtering implies that the library creates a continuous stream of information, both from acquisitions and from network sources. This stream is passed though a filtering device which selects appropriate items for individual users, based on their profiles. Filtering can be based on subject relevance, but also on other considerations such as level, source type, language and quality. especially in the area of quality filtering, appropriate criteria and filtering methods will have to be developed. Information filtering is especially suited for dynamic information streams such as found on the Internet. This area is currently being studied in the Borges Project under the European Commission's Telematics for Libraries Programme.

0.9   Workplace integration

Workplace integration is a more far-reaching concept. aimed at providing the user with an integrated networked information environment for searching, retrieving, processing, creating and publishing information. It combines networked services offered by the library with sophisticated software available at the user's desktop. An example of this concept is the 'Advanced Information Workstation (AIW)' currently being developed by the Kninklijke Bibliotheek in the Netherlands. The functionality of the AIW can be described as follows:

- navigation services for identifying both printed and electronic knowledge resources;
- access services for downloading resources from network locations, entering loan requests to an on-line library service, etc. An accounting system is available for managing access to fee-based services (e.g. commercial databases) to which the library subscribes;
- software for office functions (e.g. personal database, word processing, DTP);
- software for (networked) publishing.

Workplace integration requires sophisticated technical resources such as client-server software (providing integration at the client level rather than at the server level) software integration (such as OLE under Windows) and data integration (transparent interchange of data between applications).

8. Maintaining the quality of knowledge mediation in the networked environment

8.1 Quality of resources

In performing its knowledge mediation function, the library acts as a 'window' to available knowledge resources. Through its resource discovery mechanisms, it offers the user a view on resources which are relevant to his or her information needs. However, the user expects more from the library than assistance in the selection of materials which relate to the subject matter of the information need. Relevance has wider implications than subject matter alone. It also includes issues of quality. In other words, users expect that the window provided by the library offers a view on resources which are of the highest quality pertinent to their information needs.

Traditionally, quality control of resources is achieved in a number of ways:

- by publishers through the process of peer review and editorial control;

- by libraries through selective acquisition of high quality resources;

- by the user through the use of reviews, bibliographies and references from colleagues etc.

In summary: if a resource has been published by a reputable publisher, if it has been selected for acquisition by a competent library, and/or if it as been referred to by a professional in the field, the user has a good indication that it has sufficient quality to merit some consideration.

In the dynamic network environment, these mechanisms often do not work anymore:

- many - currently in fact most - networked resources are published without any form of peer review or editorial control;

- network tools provide access to resources which have not been specifically selected by the library and of which, in fact, the library may have no prior knowledge;

- the speed and volume of network publishing makes timely and comprehensive coverage of resources by reviews etc. almost impossible.

The consequence of this is that networked resources include a relatively small number of high quality materials hidden in a vast amount of low quality, often even unreliable resources, and that it is extremely difficult to single out high quality materials without being swamped by the low quality materials as well.

Here lies an opportunity for libraries to provide added value in a way which is in fact at the heart of the traditional library function, namely *pre-selection*. In the context of printed publications the library adds quality control to it knowledge mediation by selecting publications for acquisition that are not only relevant to the subject domain of its users' needs, but also meet certain quality requirements. This type of quality control can be applied to networked resources in exactly the same manner.

There are two ways in which pre-selection can be applied to networked resources:

- By downloading high quality resources to a local server. This effectively amounts to 'electronic acquisition'.

- By maintaining (or providing links to) electronic lists of high quality resources or to servers which themselves apply quality standards to the documents they include. Such lists can be maintained as Gopher menus or WWW pages.

In both cases the library acts as a quality filter, restricting access to resources of known quality. It is clear, of course, that this type of restriction will not be welcomed by all users. They may wish to make their own quality decisions, or they might argue that pre-selection will of necessity miss some relevant materials (this discussion of recall versus precision applies to quality selection as well as to subject retrieval). Users should therefore be given the option to enter the entire network resource space, but would be made aware of the quality problems involved in doing so.

Libraries will have to develop their own quality guidelines for networked resources. These may differ, depending on the subject domain, type of library and users, etc. For instance, in an academic environment the library might focus on reviewed materials and non-reviewed materials from well-known authors. In a business library, quality may be defined more in terms of timeliness and quality of source (e.g. press agencies, important companies).

Because of the lack of peer review, libraries may have to draw more on the expertise of professionals in specific domains for assessing the quality of networked resources. Other approaches to assessing the quality of networked resources are:

- identifying sources of peer reviewed materials (e.g. from official publishers);

- drawing from lists, reviews etc. maintained by others specifically for identifying high quality materials.

The role of libraries in enhancing the quality of networked information should not be underestimated. Whereas a great deal of current network access is carried out on an individual basis by users at their desktop, the library offers a controlled environment where a body of experience and expertise with network use and the quality issues involved can be built up. Libraries should attempt to consolidate and share such expertise, and communicate it to the larger network community. In that way, the quality judgements and the volume of use of resources *in libraries* can even serve as a statistical indicator of quality. In order to enhance this role, a certain level of organisation is required. A number of suggestions to do this are:

- developing procedures for recording experience with and quality assessments of networked resources, resource sites, network publishers etc. in the library; this should include both experience of library personnel and feedback from users;

- developing mechanisms for communicating and sharing expertise, e.g. through list servers, resource assessment databases etc.;

- conferences and workshops between librarians and with other parties involved in the networks in order to share experience and develop quality control mechanisms.

A final aspect to be discussed in this context is that of quality indicators attached to networked resources. At the present moment, references to networked resources are usually in the form of a uniform resource locator (URL) which identifies the name, location, type and access method of a resource. A URL provides only access information. It does not provide any data that can be used for identifying and selecting resources on specific criteria such as subject or quality. Work is now being carried out on the development of uniform resource characteristics (URC), i.e. a set of data elements which describe various aspects of the individual resource[11]. This would at

---

[11]   Cf. Appendix 1, section 0.

least make it easier to select documents on the basis of authors, issuing organisations, editorial status, cost etc. It is even possible that in future the URC could include an indication of quality, e.g. an indication that the resource is peer-reviewed. This will, of course, depend on a role of intermediary bodies (e.g. publishers, review boards) to provide a quality assessment. Although these developments are highly important, they as yet do not offer a solution to the problem of quality assessment and selection in libraries.

8.2 Quality of network access

An second quality issue relevant to networked resources is the quality of access. There are various aspects to this issue.

Access to networked resources is provided through network tools such as Gopher clients and WWW-browsers. These tools can either be available in the library or at the user's own desktop. Many such tools are in the public domain (shareware), but commercial versions are often also available. In order to maintain quality in this area, libraries should take care to obtain well-tested commercial versions of network tools. They also have to keep in mind that new versions of such tools are frequently brought out. Libraries should attempt to obtain the most recent versions, since creators of networked resources tend to make use of new features incorporated in such tools. The same applies to viewers used in combination with network access tools for accessing specific resource formats (e.g. image, sound and video files, as well as document formats such as postscript or Adobe).

Quality of the network infrastructure is another aspect. This includes both the speed of network access and delivery, and the availability of the network and network sites. If pre-selection of network sites (where important resources are located) is offered, the library should choose reliable sites with sufficient capacity to cope with the expected volume of use. In general, sites which are geographically close to the library should be chosen in order to maximise speed and minimise network load (alternative sites often exist, since many resources are 'mirrored' on a number of different sites). Another way to increase quality of access is to download important and frequently used resources to a local server.

Although many aspects of network speed and availability are outside the control of the library, the library should at least chose a reliable network access provider with sufficient capacity and network bandwidth. If the library provides access to electronic resources on local or institutional networks (e.g. networked CD-ROMs), care should be taken to provide sufficient network and computer capacity to handle peak-time use and expected increase of use in order to avoid user irritation.

A final aspect is the quality of links to resources. This is a difficult area, since many links in resource spaces such as Gopher and the WWW are unreliable, e.g. due to typing errors, or because of changes in the availability or version of resources which are not correctly reflected in the links. Links on the network itself are beyond the control of the library and are difficult to predict or correct. Links created in the library (e.g. in bibliographic descriptions of networked documents included in the OPAC, or on resource lists set up by the library) should be checked periodically. In fact, systematic checking of links to resources should be considered as an important aspect of quality control in the networked library.

9. Language issues in the networked environment

An extremely important problem - related to the quality issues described in section 0 - in the context of European libraries is the issue of language. The problem applies predominantly to networked resources, since English is the main language used on the global networks. Although an increasing number of documents in national languages are now being put on the Internet, the problem remains how to identify these within the huge volume of English language materials. Libraries, and especially their users, encounter major problems in dealing with this situation in so far as they are not fluent in English, as is the case in many European countries.

The language problem concerns two specific areas: the language of networked resources, and the language of discovery mechanisms and network tools.

When a library acquires resources for internal storage, or provides access to resources on the network by means of pre-selection, users can be isolated from resources in languages they do not understand. Even then, the librarian is left with the problem of having to identify resources in the appropriate language. Perhaps one has to conclude that for the present being 'network librarians' need to have sufficient command of English.

When a library in a non-English speaking country provides general access to resource spaces on the network, the library has no control over the language of materials offered to users, and they too have to find their way through a mass of information which is mainly unintelligible.

A future solution will be found in the inclusion of language codes in the URC (i.e. descriptive characteristics attached to networked resources) which can be used for selection by browsers and index and search tools. Unfortunately, developments in this area are still insufficiently advanced to offer a practical solution in the short term[12]. This area is also difficult since there is little involvement of non-English language countries in Europe in the standardisation process under which the URC and other systems for embedded metadata (descriptive data attached to networked resources) are developed. There is therefore relatively little 'push' towards standards which incorporate solutions for the multilingual problem.

---

[12]   It is therefore to be recommended that European library organisations and the European Commission stress the importance of language identification, and stimulate efforts in this direction in the network community.

It is not only the language of information resources that poses a problem. We also find that most of the tools currently used for network access (browsers, viewers, index and search tools) are based on the English language. This leads to a number of characteristics which are problematic in the context of European languages:

- In most cases the user interfaces of network tools are in English; translated versions are not available for all European languages.
- The same applies to documentation and help files which assist the users of these tools.
- In most cases the character sets of these tools cannot handle the wide range of characters used in European languages.
- Networked resource discovery mechanisms provide no mechanism for language selection, as indicated above.
- Searching for resources (using network indexes) with non-English keywords leads to inappropriate results: they may not be found (e.g. due to problems with character sets) or they may not select the language intended (e.g. the word 'information' is the same in many languages).

There is at least a need for developing tools which are better adapted to the multilingual context which meet requirements such as multilingual interfaces and help-files, multilingual character sets and, in future, automatic language filtering[13].

It should be noted, however, that the inclusion of language codes in embedded metadata and the development of tools which can cope with non-English character sets will not solve many problems with which users are now being confronted. Especially the emerging search mechanisms on the Internet (such as Yahoo, Lycos, WebCrawler etc.) are in general developed in and for the English speaking world. They do not take the problem of different languages into account. A solution would require the incorporation of Language Engineering methods and the application of linguistic resources such as lexica, dictionaries, multilingual thesauri etc. Efforts in this area do exists, such as the ISO-5964 standard for multilingual thesauri and various projects under the Telematics Programme (e.g. TRANSLIB and KANAL-S under the Libraries Programme). However, the problem is also related to policy. The developers of search mechanisms and tools, mainly based in the United States, do not view the language

---

[13]   In the desk research carried out for phase 1 of this project, we have identified at least one company (Alis Technologies) involved in developing a WWW browser which is intended to meet these requirements. (Cf http://alis.ca:8082/).

problem as sufficiently important to incorporate such solutions into their database applications. There is therefore a need for European search mechanisms which do take these issues into account.

In order to profit from developments in language technology, the library world could benefit from participation in the European Commission's activities in this area, both within the Telematics Programme and within the new Multilingual Information Society (MLIS) Programme which has been approved recently by the Commission. In addition, additional specific actions in this area will be required from European libraries in these programmes.

It should be emphasised that the language issue is not a marginal problem. It is an issue which, if unresolved, will impede the development of networked library services in large areas of Europe, and which will therefore prevent libraries in these areas from continuing and improving their role as knowledge mediators in the information society. It is therefore an issue of strategic importance for the European library community and their users.

10. Bibliographic control of networked resources

10.1 The expanded concept of bibliographic description

The process of bibliographic control involves the creation of descriptions of information resources in terms of their formal characteristics, subject content, location etc. These descriptions - traditionally called *bibliographic* descriptions - are organised in such a way that they can be ordered and retrieved on the basis of these characteristics, and that the descriptive elements are presented in a standard and logical way. Resource descriptions are at the core of resource discovery mechanisms, since they are used to represent resources during the discovery process. For instance, it is conceptually well-established that in a library catalogue the bibliographic description, e.g. of a printed publication, is a representation of that publication which during the search process acts as a substitute for the document itself.

For the user, a resource description is the answer provided by the resource discovery mechanism to the question: >where can I find knowledge on subject x=?[14] The answer provided by the resource mechanism is a description of and a reference or pointer to one or more information *objects* which are expected to satisfy the user's information need.

Traditionally the range of such objects was rather limited, mainly including printed publications such as monographs, reference and bibliographic works, and journal titles. It should be noted that even in the traditional library context the user does not expect a bibliographic description (e.g. a catalogue entry) always to refer to a resource (e.g. a book or article) that directly satisfies the information need. In many cases the reference is to an >entry point= in a chain of objects which eventually leads the user to relevant resources. For instance, an entry in the catalogue might refer to a bibliography which refers to a review publication which refers to an article which gives the author=s address. The user calls the author and obtains the desired information. In this case, the original resource (the bibliography) did not provide the desired information, but without this reference as an entry point, the information would not have been found.

In the network environment, one finds extensive use of such chains, which can be followed at great speed if the right tools and network capacity are available. Using

---

[14] Or, of course, related questions such as: >where can I find a copy of edition A of book B, written by C, published by D in year E=.

resource discovery mechanisms such as Gopher or WWW, a user may traverse a large number of sub-menus or links, visiting different resources from a variety of organisations and types of systems all over the world, before arriving at, say, an important recent study. A direct reference to that important study would provide the best service to that user, but this is of course not always available. Therefore, references to appropriate entry points to the resource space, e.g. references to file servers (FTP-sites), gophers, WWW-home pages, on-line databases etc. are necessary to help the user get on his way.

We can conclude therefore that bibliographic data describes objects which lead the user to relevant information resources. Any object which performs this function, can be included in the bibliographic system. In the networked library the range of such objects is much larger than in the traditional library. It includes:

- printed documents held in the library or available from other libraries
- electronic documents held in the library
- networked documents
- file servers
- Gophers
- WWW home-pages
- network indexes
- networked library and publisher catalogues
- on-line database services
- document delivery services

etc.

References to all these different types of objects can be included in a resource discovery system. It is of course possible to develop distinct resource discovery mechanisms for various types of resources. We have already pointed to the fact that users are confronted with an increasing number of discovery mechanisms divided by resource type. However, we have also argued in favour of integrated resource discovery mechanisms as a means of reducing complexity (cf. section 0). Libraries should realise that this will have major consequences for the concept of a library *catalogue*, especially when it is an automated catalogue, e.g. an OPAC.

If we regard the catalogue as the main resource discovery system for libraries, it will therefore have to include the diverse types of objects in an integrated way. What we then arrive at, is something very different from what we traditionally regard as a library catalogue. This means that traditional concepts pertaining to bibliographic control are no longer sufficient in the networked environment. Most notably, we have to abandon the idea that catalogues and bibliographic control are concerned with describing *documents*. In the network environment bibliographic control is concerned with *information resources*. This is a much wider concept, and includes any object (document, service, tool, organisation etc.) which leads the user to the desired knowledge.

On the network, accessing a computer service, database, library catalogue or whatever is as easy and quite similar to accessing a document. Ultimately, it is all information which either contains required knowledge or refers to other information containing or referring to required knowledge. There is no reason why the information resources described in the catalogue should be restricted to documents (even if we were able to define what a document is in the context of dynamic and distributed networked resources).

To give an example: a user who needs specialised information in a certain subject domain and who is willing to pay for such information, could be referred to a commercial database provider who accepts payment by credit card or a network payment method. In an integrated network environment, such a reference could be the result of a search question (>where can I find information on...=), and connection with the database could be established automatically once the user accepts to follow the reference and agrees with the (financial and legal) conditions which apply.

This example also shows that new types of descriptive data elements can be necessary in order to provide advanced networked mediation. In this case the description of the knowledge resource (a commercial database) would have to include data on cost, payment method and perhaps legal conditions. This data could be used in two ways:

- ex ante: the user indicates whether or not the discovery mechanism should select resources which incur additional costs;

- ex post: the results of the discovery process contain an indication of the cost of resources; the user uses that data to decide whether or not to access the resource.

10.2 Bibliographic description of networked resources

Apart from the need to integrate descriptions of various types of information resources in the library catalogue, there remains the issue of how to describe these resources (e.g. data elements, coding, presentation), and how to include them in existing systems and formats.

Many efforts are currently being made to develop guidelines for cataloguing electronic, networked resources. This is commonly done in the context of projects aimed at developing catalogues of networked resources and/or integrating networked resources in the library catalogue[15].

Even though guidelines now exist for cataloguing electronic resources, there remains a problem in deriving the descriptive elements from these resources. Printed publications contain a title page and often also a CIP-entry. This is a yet not the case with most electronic resources.

For electronic publications three main sources of descriptive information can be used:

- the initial screen ('title screen') shown when the publication is accessed, or any other part of the publication proper;
- embedded metadata (structured descriptive information) included with the publication;
- descriptive information on the previous access node;
- accompanying materials in electronic form (e.g. 'read-me' files);
- other accompanying materials (e.g. packaging, manuals).

There is of course a need for standardisation of various elements of electronic resources, and developments towards Universal Resource Characteristics which would be attached to resources will in future provide solution. At that time, many descriptive elements will be derived from the embedded metadata in the resources themselves. To a large extent, this could be done automatically, i.e. software will be able to 'translate' the embedded metadata into an appropriate bibliographic entry in the cataloguing system being used.

---

[15]   Some examples are given in section 4.2 of the Interim report on Phase 1: desk research of this project.

It is clear that there is no accepted standard for embedded metadata at the present moment, and that it will take at least a number of years before such a standard exists and is generally accepted and used. Issues to be decided include:

- definition of elements (e.g. author, title, etc.)
- definition of schemes (formal designators for data elements)
- syntax/format (the formal representation and structure of metadata)
- relationship with document (e.g. do embedded metadata take the form of a document header, title page or other)

For the present being therefore, cataloguers will have to apply cataloguing guidelines to resources manually, and create and share experience on how to do so in the best way.

The overall trend in cataloguing electronic publications is to treat them as far as possible in the same way as more traditional, printed publications. The specific problems of new media and publication types are handled in extensions to existing cataloguing rules. The most difficult area, and the one where most activity is taking place, is that of on-line networked resources.

The current practice can be summarised as follows:

- Cataloguing rules for software and data on diskettes are already available[16]. These rules provide guidelines which can be applied to other types of off-line media as well.

- Existing cataloguing rules and bibliographic formats have been adapted and extended to accommodate electronic and networked materials. Examples are various extensions to the USMarc format (e.g. field 856 for access data) and changes to the PICA format as a result of the DocServer Project.

- Work has also been done on bibliographic control of interactive multimedia which can be regarded as a specific type of electronic publication[17]. This work has

---

[16]   Cf AACR (2nd ed., 1988 revision - chapter 9: computer files) and ISBD(CF). ISBD(CF) is currently in the process of revision.

[17]   The ALA definition of interactive multimedia is 'a media residing on one or more physical carriers or on a computer network, which employs user controlled, nonlinear navigation using computer technology and combines two or more media (audio, images, text, graphics, animation or media) that the user manipulates to control the order and/or nature of the presentation. Cf Swanekamp, J. - Interactive multimedia: issues for bibliographic control. - Paper presented at the Seminar on Cataloguing Digital

resulted, *inter alia*, in The Guidelines for Bibliographic Description of Interactive Multimedia by the American Library Association, Chicago, in 1994. Interactive multimedia are currently entered as computer files by OCLC and RLIN, but discussions are underway to develop a new byte in the MARC leader and a new 008 for these materials.

- New standards are being developed for specific areas and/or to assist information providers in creating descriptive metadata. Examples include:

  - the Text Encoding Initiative for the digital encoding of texts in the humanities, which has developed a set of metadata (the 'TEI header') for descriptive information;

  - the IETF Working group on Document Identifiers which is developing a standard for Uniform Resource Characteristics (URCs) to represent metadata;

  - the so-called 'Dublin Core Metadata Set' proposed at the OCLC/NCSA Metadata Workshop in March 1995, offering a basic but extensible set of descriptive elements for networked resources.

- In addition to these various 'formal' attempts to develop standards and guidelines for metadata and cataloguing, many hands-on activities are being carried out which add to a body of common practice in this area. One can distinguish three types of activities:

  - Large scale projects and pilots aimed at developing catalogues of electronic resources; examples include the British Catriona project and OCLC's 'Catalog of Internet Resources' project in the US[18].

  - Index services which are more or less 'built into' the Internet, such as Alex, Lycos, WebCrawler and Yahoo. These effectively function as 'catalogues' or 'databases' of networked resources offering increasingly sophisticated

Documents, Washington, Library of Congress, October 1994.
[http://lcweb.loc.gov/catdir/semdigdocs/joan.html]

[18] A useful outcome of this project is the document 'Cataloguing Internet resources: a manual and practical guide' edited by Nancy B. Olson (OCLC, 1995) [http://www.oclc.org/oclc/man/9256cat/toc.htm]. This document discusses the use of AACR2 (notably section 9) for cataloguing networked resources. It provides the best practical guidelines available at this time, and should be used as the basis for cataloguing deposited materials.

retrieval functions; their major deficiency is the lack of informative metadata: the description of documents returned as a result of an index search is usually inadequate to judge their relevance.

- Domain-oriented lists, gopher structures and WWW-pages which provide descriptions of important resources in a certain subject field, geographic area, profession etc.; these lists are usually created by individuals, libraries and professional institutions.

An increasing number of guidelines for citing electronic publications in reference lists and bibliographies is being published[19].

An important issue is of course how to include the new electronic resource types in the existing catalogue system. The approach most commonly taken, is to include as many elements as possible in existing fields in the bibliographic format, e.g. author, title, publisher etc. Problems arise, of course, with elements which are specific for a certain resource type and are not explicitly covered by the bibliographic format. The most important area for networked resources is 'access data', i.e. data on the resource type or 'access method' (e.g. an FTP-file, gopher or HTML document), its network location (e.g. the URL) and its document format (e.g. ASCII or postscript format). This can either be handled by extending the format with new fields, or by using existing fields explicitly for this purpose. For systems using the MARC format, it has become common to use the 856-field to include this type of data (Figure 7).[20]

---

[19]   Examples are:
Patrias, K. - National Library of Medicine recommended formats for bibliographic citation. - Bethesda, NLM, 1991. (Chapter 12: Electronic information formats).
Li, X. ; Crane, N.B. - Electronic style: a guide to citing electronic information. - Westport: Meckler, 1993.
[20]   A more extensive discussion of bibliographic control of electronic publications will be contained in the Final Report of the ELDEP study of issues faced by national libraries in the field of deposit collections of electronic publications by NBBI. This report will be published by the European Commission early in 1996.

A recent set of guidelines for including access data in the USMarc record is published in: Guidelines for the use of field 856 / Library of Congress, Network Development and MARC Standards Office, March 1995. The following overview of the structure of field 856 is derived from this document:

First Indicator (defines use of rest of field):

        0   E-mail
        1   FTP
        2   Remote Login (Telnet)
        3   Dial-up
        7   Method specified in subfield $2

Subfield codes:

$a   Host name (network address)
$b   Access number (e.g. IP address, telephone number)
$c   Compression information
$d   Path (directories)
$f   Electronic name (filename)
$g   Electronic name - End of range (for set of files)
$h   Processor of request (data preceding @)
$i   Instruction (command to host for processing of request)
$j   Bits per second (lowest and highest transmission speed)
$k   Password (for access to resource)
$l   Logon/logout
$m   Contact for access assistance
$n   Name of location of host in subfield $a
$o   Operating system
$p   Port (of process or service in host)

$q   File transfer method (e.g. ASCII or binary)
$r   Settings (Data bits, stop bits, parity)
$s   File size
$t   Terminal emulation (e.g. VT102)
$u   Uniform Resource Locator (combination of various other subfields)
$v   Hours access method available
$w   Record control number
$x   Non-public note (for library use)
$z   Public note
$2   Access method (other than in Indicator 1, e.g. http)
$3   Materials specified

Figure 7: USMARC Field 856

Whichever solution is used, one has to keep in mind that access data has a dual function in the bibliographic resource discovery system. On the one hand, it has to be structured in such a way that it can be presented to and interpreted by the user who consults the catalogue and wishes to make a note of the way to access the resource. On the other hand, if network access is an integrated component of the catalogue, it is necessary that the system can interpret the data in order to access the resource on the network. In simple terms: the access data has to be passed on to a network browser software which is called when the user indicates he would like to access the networked document described in the catalogue. This also means that the data has to be presented to the user in such a way that it he or she can make an appropriate decision whether or not to access the resource through the network.

It has to be stressed that references to network locations (e.g. URLs) are particularly sensitive to errors, either due to typing mistakes or to changes in the network location. As described in section 0, this is an important issue for bibliographic quality control and maintenance.

At the present moment libraries tend to accommodate bibliographic control of and access to networked resources within the constraints of existing cataloguing rules, bibliographic formats and library catalogue systems. There is of course a pragmatic reason for this, since it requires relatively little change in familiar practices and procedures, and requires a low investment in systems. But in the long run these solutions will not be satisfactory: they provide little support for the complicated task of networked cataloguing, and offer the user less functionality, ease of use and support than might be expected at the current state of technology. There is therefore a future need for a new generation of library systems. These should be designed to cope with the requirements of integrated networked services. They will also have to be sufficiently open and flexible to accommodate the many changes and new developments which will be inevitable in the network environment during the next decade.

Cataloguing electronic networked resources - and maintaining the quality of the bibliographic record - is therefore a difficult and expensive task. Benefits in this area can be found in sharing the task between libraries, e.g. on a national or subject domain It should be noted that even when a library integrates descriptions of networked resources in the catalogue, it will probably also use other ways to provide bibliographic references of networked resources to users. For instance, a library's Gopher or WWW server may include lists of (links to) resources of special interest, e.g. in specific subject domains. If one looks at the vast amount of such lists already available on the Internet - often created outside the library world - it becomes clear that the descriptions on these lists are usually not up to the standards which are common in the word of bibliography. Libraries should take care to adhere to bibliographic standards (e.g. ISBD) in describing resources on their own lists, thereby providing an example of good practice to the network community. Explicit links to network locations (URLs) should always be added to bibliographic descriptions, not only on WWW pages but also on Gopher menu entries and text files containing descriptions of networked resources.

11. User support for knowledge mediation

11.1 Support methods

Using networked resources is not only new to libraries, it is also new to their users. It is therefore essential that libraries think carefully about the way they can support the users of networked library services. This is a difficult area, since there is hardly a body of experience on which to draw, and because the network skills of users are divers and changing. The latter reason leads to the complicating factor that libraries will have to develop different levels of support adapted to the level of skills of the individual user.

In general, one can distinguish the following methods for providing user support in the context of networked library services:

- *personal assistance* through face-to-face contact between user and librarian;

- *distance support* (by telephone or e-mail) from a help-desk;

- *printed manuals*, ranging from general introductions for using the library or the Internet, to detailed manuals for using a specific system or search tool;

- *resource guides*, e.g. structured and annotated lists of resources or resource areas which help the user to select resources in a specific domain, and if necessary provide information on how to obtain these resources; in the networked environment these can often be set up as Gopher menu structures or WWW pages;

- *signposting,* i.e. visual clues which help the user to find their way through the library and find appropriate resource, access and support areas; for networked access to the library, a top-level interface can be developed which consists of a 'map' or other visualisation of the library which the user can use to access various library functions;

- *on-screen instructions* included as a component of the user interface of applications such as library systems and search tools;

- *electronic help files*, callable from applications, preferably providing context sensitive help (i.e. related to the task currently being carried out);

- *user instruction:* in many cases the best way to support users is to instruct and train them in order that they have sufficient background knowledge and skills to use the library without or with a limited amount of further assistance; especially when networked services are introduced, additional user instruction becomes necessary;

- *computerised training aids* are additional support tools which can help the user to acquire the required skills; there are many possibilities in this area, including interactive training (for instance for using browsers or hypertext) and practice databases.

- *resource descriptions:* although not generally recognised as an aspect of user support, the descriptive data of knowledge resources provided by discovery mechanisms is of course extremely important in assisting the user to select appropriate resources; enhanced bibliographic descriptions, the inclusion of abstracts, contents pages, reviews, data on quality, cost, availability etc. all help the user to select resources that best meet their information needs; especially in the networked environment, resource description is not only necessary for bibliographic control but also for increasing the effectiveness of knowledge mediation.

The networked library should try to provide the entire range of support methods, finding an effective balance between the various options, depending on user needs.

It should be noted that some systems provide 'electronic' support (e.g. on-screen instructions and help files) that can be adapted to the level of skills of the individual user (e.g. novice or advanced user). Some systems allow the library to adapt on-screen instructions and/or help files for their own needs. These aspects could be used as criteria for deciding which system or tool should be acquired for use in the library. Systems even exist which adapt automatically to the level of experience of the user; these are however of little use in a library environment where an application is used by a large number of different users.

Unfortunately, the library cannot control all of the support methods listed above. personal assistance, help desks, manuals, guidelines and signposting can be developed by the library and adapted to user needs. This is not always the case with on-line support provided by systems. In many cases, especially with current network tools, user support is defined by the supplier; the library cannot always change the user interface with its embedded instructions or help files. Elsewhere we have noted that these tools also often create a language problem (e.g. they are only available in English). In these cases, the library will have to add other methods, such as its own manuals (in the appropriate languages) and/or personal assistance.

Libraries have to plan, develop and maintain a comprehensive support function for networked services as an extension to the existing support function. It is recommended that they do this in a stepwise way. The use of networked services, and the problems that users have in this area have to be monitored carefully and on a continuing basis. A periodic review of support needs has to be made and the support functions has to be adapted to the problems and needs identified. This is another area where libraries can share experience and expertise, and where methods such as described in section 0 are appropriate.

11.2 Support for networked knowledge mediation

In the previous paragraph we have discussed a number of *methods* for providing support to users. In this section we identify the various points in the knowledge mediation process where specific types of support are needed from the viewpoint of the user. These can be used as checkpoints for monitoring the need for and effectiveness of user support.

The following are the most important points where users typically require support.

11.2.1 Choice of resource type

In many cases, a specific knowledge need can best be served by one or more specific resource types, e.g. a monograph, journal article, newspaper, on-line database, networked resource etc. In some cases, referring the user to a person or organisation is more appropriate. User instruction is an appropriate way to provide users with the background knowledge to handle this type of decision. Also, a user guide should be developed, setting out the various options, describing the range of resources available in and through the library (including networked resources) and criteria for choosing appropriate types for different types of knowledge needs. For specific cases, personal assistance and/or a networked help desk has to be available.

11.2.2 Choice of discovery mechanism

A next choice the user has to make, is that of the appropriate discovery mechanism. As indicated in section 0, the choice of resource mechanism can influence the range of resources which the user can find through that mechanism. There is therefore a relationship with the choice of resource type, depending on the level of integration offered by the library. The same support methods as in the previous paragraph can be used here. Manuals and other instructive materials should advise users on the appropriate discovery mechanisms for various types of resources.

11.2.3 Use of discovery mechanism

Using a resource discovery mechanism involves two important support issues:

- Support for using the functions of the resource discovery *system*, i.e. the catalogue, on-line or CD-ROM based database, network browser etc. User instruction, printed manuals, on-line help and personal assistance are appropriate support methods. Adequate interface design also enhances the ease of use.

- Support for identifying relevant *knowledge resources*. Most modern resource discovery mechanisms combine aspects of *searching* and *browsing*. Searching involves the use of search terms (author names, title words, classification codes, subject keywords etc.). Users often need assistance for translating information needs into effective search profiles, choosing the right search terms, using Boolean logic etc. Instruction, manuals, on-screen help and personal assistance are all necessary support methods for this area.

Browsing typically involves a number of steps which reduce the set of available resources to a subset which can be scanned for relevant information. In most discovery mechanisms this is achieved by choosing subsequent sub-areas of the information space. For instance, when browsing the Internet, the user might first choose a specific networked resource space such as FTP, Gopher or WWW. From the initial entry point into the resource space (e.g. FTP site, Gopher main menu or WWW home page) the user may choose a subsection (e.g. a directory, menu item or WWW link), and so forth. Ultimately, the user arrives either at a single document, or at a set of documents from which to choose. If the required information does not (fully) satisfy the information need, the user can 'backtrack' to a higher level and choose a different branch which, hopefully, will lead to other, useful information.

In many cases, more detailed advice can be given for the choice of areas within a resource space. Based on the library's knowledge of and experience with networked information, guidelines for choosing specific useful library catalogues, on-line databases, FTP sites (e.g. document servers), Gophers and WWW pages for various subject domains or other information needs can be developed. These guidelines or resource lists can be made available in electronic form, e.g. on the library's Gopher of WWW pages. This is in fact the pre-selection function for networked access (cf. sections 0 and 0).

Other methods for supporting browsing are user instruction, manuals and personal assistance. Another important method is provided by the level of detail given by resource descriptions in the catalogue and on resource lists. Enhanced descriptions are also, of course, important to help the user decide whether individual knowledge resources found through resource discovery mechanisms (either by searching or by browsing) do indeed meet the user's information needs. Unfortunately, this is beyond the control of the library for resource descriptions on the network which are not created by the library itself (cf. section 0).

11.2.4 Resource location

Many resource discovery systems identify knowledge resources without specifying their location, i.e. without telling the user exactly where he or she can obtain the resource. This is, of course, true for traditional bibliographic publications and databases which describe resources within a certain domain without reference to physical collections. After identifying a resource the user then has to locate it, for instance by checking it against the library catalogue. Networked reference resources which serve to identify electronic knowledge resources on the network usually contain direct links to these resources, in which case location is no problem. However, many networked reference resources, varying from authors' publication lists to networked on-line databases, refer at least in part to printed, non-networked publications. This can be confusing to users; they may have difficulty in understanding why some resources can be accessed directly over the network, while other resources cannot, nor provide any clue where they might be obtained. Network users will tend to neglect non-networked knowledge resources if the library does not support them in locating and accessing these materials.

In addition to obvious support methods such as instruction, on-screen help and personal assistance, libraries should try to support the location of resources through technical measures. In general these involve mechanisms which automatically link resource descriptions to location and access data (cf. section 0.3).

11.2.5 Selection of alternative resources, locations, forms and delivery methods

At all the various steps involved in finding and obtaining knowledge resources, the user is confronted with alternative options and therefore a number of choices:

- the choice of resource discovery mechanism, e.g. go directly to the library catalogue, consult a printed or electronic bibliography, browse through the network or use a network search mechanism;
- a choice between alternative resource forms, if available (e.g. printed or electronic form, CD-ROM, on-line database or networked hypertext document, etc.);
- a choice between alternative locations for obtaining the resource (e.g. via ILL or a commercial document provider, from the library or directly from the network, from alternative networks locations)
- a choice between alternative delivery options

Perhaps the most fundamental - and to users the most confusing - choice is that between alternative resource discovery mechanisms, since this directly influences the result and success of finding relevant knowledge resources (cf. chapter 6). The choice between alternative resource forms is related to personal preferences and/or differences between these forms for a specific resource. Choices between alternative locations and delivery options are especially related to issues concerning speed and cost. In all cases, the library will have to offer the user guidance in choosing between alternatives.

Examples of practical decisions with which users are confronted are outlined in Figure 8. The library should help the user to understand these alternatives and assist them in making the best choice in different situations.

Choice	Alternatives	Decision criteria
Form of information resource	- Print - Electronic	- Currency / coverage - Cost - Ease of use
Accessing database on CD-ROM or on-line host	- CD-ROM - On-line database	- Currency / coverage - Update frequency - Cost - Ease of use
Alternative network resource spaces	- FTP - Gopher - WWW	- Resource type - Document size - Download/print or viewing
Choice of network browsing method	- Multipurpose (e.g. WWW-browser) - Specific (e.g. FTP or Gopher client)	- Functionality - Ease of use
Choice of network search mechanism	- Resource specific mechanisms (Archie, Veronica, Wais) - Various general services (Yahoo, WebCrawler, Lycos, etc.)	- Currency / coverage - Functionality - Speed - Cost (for commercial search services)
Alternative network locations	- Multiple URLs	- Geographic distance to server - Network congestion
Transfer method	- On-site consultation viewing - Loan / photocopy - Fax - Mail (normal or electronic) - Fax	- Type of resource - Type of use - Speed of delivery - Cost of delivery

Figure 8: User decisions

11.2.6 Handling of electronic resources

The steps described so far are all concerned with the process of identifying, locating and obtaining knowledge resources. We have already discussed the fact that in the networked library this process may be different and more complicated than in the traditional library. But that is not all. The knowledge resources which are the outcome of this process, are more and more *electronic* documents obtained from networked sources. It is an understatement to say that the handling of electronic resources is different from the handling of printed resources. Consulting a hypertext document, viewing and printing documents, filing them on a personal computer, or taking advantage of copying and editing references, citations etc. electronically are examples of skills which users need to acquire and of activities which the library will have to support. In other words: the library should not only support users in their role of information seekers, but also in their role as information users. User instruction, computerised training aids and personal instruction are appropriate support methods in this area.

12. Networked relations with publishers

12.1 Electronic distribution from publishers to libraries

Libraries are increasingly establishing relations with publishers for acquiring materials (especially journals) in electronic form. Many if not most of these activities do not pertain to electronic publications or networked resources in the strict sense. Rather, the object if to achieve electronic distribution of traditional resources to the library, and to provide on-line access to these materials for end users. This in fact amounts to an alternative distribution method for traditional, printed journals.

A well-known example is the TULIP project, where a group of academic publishers distributes journals to the library on CD-ROM. The TULIP system includes retrieval software and an accounting mechanism. Users can access individual articles on the system in the library. However, the TULIP system has a number of drawbacks. The materials available are limited to a fixed set of journal titles and may not cover the full journal holdings of the library, even of the publishers involved. The system is basically stand-alone, and therefore does not allow networked remote access to the materials. Bibliographic descriptions of the materials are contained within the system, and cannot be integrated in the library's main resource discovery system, i.e. the on-line catalogue.

Recent developments are moving towards an approach whereby electronic delivery from publisher to library covers the full set of journals from a specific publisher to which the library has subscribed. There is also a move towards licensing agreements which allow on-line access to the materials for registered users. Another important aspect of these developments is that publishers are now willing to deliver bibliographic descriptions in an electronic form which allows integration into the on-line catalogue or networked databases. In summary, this is a far more flexible approach which is more in line with developments towards networked library services, and which allows the library to adapt the service to its own needs and possibilities.

Two projects in the Netherlands provide examples of this new approach. One is the agreement between the library of Tilburg University and Elsevier. Under this agreement, the Elsevier journals to which the library subscribes are delivered in image format, from which a database is created. Bibliographic data is included in SGML-format and is integrated in the on-line catalogue. networked access to the materials is allowed, taking certain restrictions and procedures into account which should prevent unfair use.

A more wide-ranging service is now being developed by PICA (the organisation responsible for the major part of the library systems and services infrastructure in the Netherlands). The service, called WebDOC, has been developed by PICA in co-operation with a number of academic libraries in the Netherlands and Germany and with commercial publishers. Its objective is to provide end-user access to journal articles in electronic form. Articles are obtained from publishers in a variety of formats (Postscript, PDF, HTML or TIFF-images) and stored on local document servers in the libraries or on a central PICA-server. Bibliographic data and abstracts are provided in the form of SGML headers for individual articles, and are stored in a networked catalogue (WebCAT) which contains hyperlinks to the full text articles. These materials can be accessed by registered users of the libraries through a WWW browser. Unlimited access is available for journal titles to which the user's library has subscribed. There is a 'pay-per-view' arrangement for accessing other titles. The WebDOC project is currently in a pilot phase, and is expected to become operational at the beginning of 1996 for a period of two years. A contract has already been signed by Kluwer Academic Publishers to participate in the pilot. Recently the WebDOC project has been expanded to include the Research Libraries Group (RLG) in the United States. The new service will allow end users to search a networked catalogue of bibliographic records via a Web browser, and to retrieve documents (including journal articles, images, maps and primary sources). WebDOC will include a licensing and accounting mechanism to control access, e.g. to verify that the user is allowed to access a document under an institutional license, or else to charge the user individually.

What is now developing is in fact a form of 'networked publishing' which puts the library in the role of providing and controlling access to publications rather than acquiring, storing and cataloguing them.[21] Again recently, Academic Press has announced a service called Ideal, which will deliver journal articles over the Internet using Adobe Acrobat. The service will deliver information directly to the users desktop pc, and will allow the user to browse tables of contents and abstracts of articles, and to search the abstracts using verity's TOPIC retrieval software. The system, based on ICL's Command software, allows administration to be delegated to libraries subscribing tot the service. In other words, only users registered at the library will obtain access. In the United Kingdom, under the Electronic Libraries Programme, a project called Superjournal involving some 21 publishers is now being set up. this project aims at providing networked access to newly created multimedia journals with

---

[21]   Cf: Superjournals address the subscriptions spiral. - In: Information world review, November 1995, no. 108.

---

video, animation and 3-dimensional graphics. Another development in this area is the integration of AT&T's RightPages system and World Wide Web browsers. This system allows users to select individual journal issues, browse through journal pages and tables of content, and to print articles. The service will not be made generally available on the Internet, but will be delivered through libraries on their own, internal networks. The reason for using WWW-technology is that many users are now familiar with using browsers such as Netscape.

12.2 Knowledge distribution strategies

If we now look at knowledge distribution and mediation from the publishers' perspective, there appear to be two possible strategies:

P = publisher

- Direct distribution to end-users (fig. 7). From a technological viewpoint, networks offer publishers the opportunity to distribute their products directly to end-users, without the intermediary function of libraries and other parties (including booksellers and subscription agents). This would, of course, mean shifting from a relatively small customer base (libraries) to a much larger one (end-users) and most probably require a shift from pre-paid subscriptions to a pay-per-use model. It would also necessitate the implementation of (networked) payment mechanisms to be used by individual users.

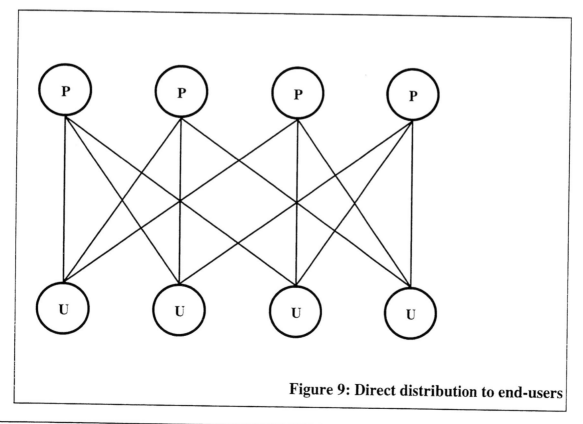

Figure 9: Direct distribution to end-users

- Distribution through intermediaries (fig. 8). This strategy copies the existing model in which intermediaries (such as libraries) act as a clearing house between a set of publishers and a set of users.

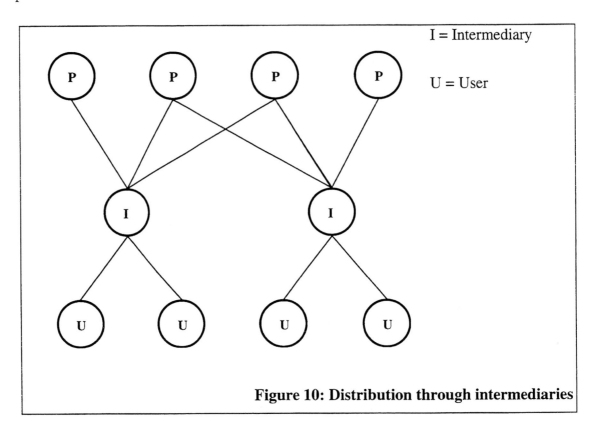

P = publisher

I = Intermediary

U = User

Figure 10: Distribution through intermediaries

Although direct relationships between publishers and users may seem an attractive benefit of network developments, it turns out to have a number of significant disadvantages:

- Handling large volumes of financial transactions with end-users is complicated and adds to the overall cost of publishing.
- Publishers will have to develop and maintain user-oriented networked retrieval systems to provide users access to materials.
- Direct distribution to end-users offers no guarantee that materials will be preserved and kept available in the long term.
- Available information is not structured on an intellectual/conceptual basis (e.g. disciplines or subjects), but on an organisational basis (i.e. by publisher).
- Users are confronted with many access points (instead of a single intermediary), probably with a conspicuous lack of uniformity in interfaces and procedures.

- Direct distribution lacks the general level of user support offered by intermediaries such as libraries.
- Publishers will not provide additional library-type services (e.g. literature searches, disciplinary-based current awareness services, selection based on quality, intellectual level etc.).

For reasons such as these, the role of intermediaries remains important, both in the interest of users and in that of publishers themselves. Although the intermediary function could be performed by types of organisations (e.g. specialised 'digital' libraries, even on a commercial basis), Existing libraries seem to be in a better position to perform this function. Arguments in favour of this view include:

- Libraries already have experience with the issues involved (e.g. selection, cataloguing and indexing, storage and preservation, user support) and have infrastructures which can be expanded towards networked services.
- Libraries already have a firm user base for which they are a recognised and familiar source of information.
- Libraries and publishers have a long history of co-operation and know each other sufficiently well to develop services together.

The case for libraries as intermediaries in the electronic distribution of publications is further strengthened by the developments described in the first part of this section. Current developments in publishing are not really moving towards new types of electronic publications, but rather towards new, electronic modes of distributing existing types of publications for which the library already acts as an intermediary. Such shifts in distribution mode are easier if carried out by existing partners, than when new actors have to be drawn in.

12.3 Library - publisher co-operation

The conclusion to be drawn from current developments is that the concept of networked services is being expanded to include 'traditional' published journals, thereby broadening the range of resources that can be distributed to users through the networks. It is also interesting to note that publishers are now beginning to regard libraries as an important link in the electronic distribution channel. They appear to prefer co-operation with libraries as a 'distribution centre', rather than offering on-line access to and maintaining an administrative relationship with individual end-users themselves. An additional advantage is that libraries can provide feedback to publishers in the form of usage data. because libraries know their users, they can more easily relate usage data to user characteristics such as academic position, subject field etc.

These developments offer libraries challenging opportunities for developing new networked services. The challenges are significant. First, the library has to innovate its technical infrastructure in order to cope with electronic publications in addition to printed materials. The importance of a co-operative library network such as PICA for providing the technical resources and for organising the relationship with publishers should not be underestimated, since it makes it much easier for individual libraries to offer this kind of service. Secondly, it puts a responsibility on the library to comply with licensing conditions and to ensure that unfair use of electronic materials does not occur. Finally, the library has to provide support to end-users in using this type of service, along the same lines as described for other networked resources.

13. Knowledge mediation and the library context

We can now relate the various decisions and activities in the knowledge mediation process as follows (Figure 11):

Action	User	Library	Process
Knowledge resources	Choose type(s) of knowledge resources to be sought	Decide which types of resources are to be made available within the library and from other sources	ACQ
		Support user in choosing appropriate resource types	US
Discovery mechanism	Choose most appropriate type of discovery mechanism(s) for knowledge-seeking task	Decide which discovery mechanisms are to be offered to the user, their integration and presentation	RCI
		Support user in choosing appropriate discovery mechanism(s)	US
Resource discovery	Identify relevant resources with chosen discovery mechanism(s)	*Support use of discovery mechanisms*	US
Resource location	Find the location of resources if not provided by the discovery mechanism	*Support locating resources, preferably through automatic mechanisms*	US
Resource selection	Select resources from those identified	*Support selection of alternative resources, resource locations and resource forms*	US
	Select appropriate location if alternatives exist		
	Select appropriate form if alternatives exist		

Action	User	Library	Process
Delivery method	Choose appropriate delivery method based on convenience, speed, cost, etc.	Decide which types of delivery methods to be made available for specific types of resources and use(rs)	LDD
		Support choice of appropriate delivery method	US
Resource provision		Create relationships with other libraries /document providers	LDD
		Choose provision method	
		Obtain the resource(s) at the library	
Resource transfer	Borrow, photocopy or download the resource	Transfer (a copy of) the resource to the user if necessary	LDD
Resource utilisation	Acquire knowledge from the resource, distribute the resource (or its embodied knowledge) to others	*Support handling of electronic resources*	US

ACQ = Acquisitions; RCI = Reference, Cataloguing & Indexing; LDD = Lending & Document Delivery;

US = User Support

Decision points	*Support functions*

Figure 11: Knowledge mediation activities

The various options outlined in this table allow for different sets of solutions, depending on available resources, level of technical facilities, library type etc. A number of solutions will be described in more detail as *application models* in part 3 of this report.

14. Key issues in knowledge mediation

From the preceding analysis we can now identify the following key issues in knowledge mediation:

- Networks have greatly expanded the range of resources to which libraries can offer their users access; at the same time, the range of tools for identifying, locating and accessing resources has also increased.

- Knowledge mediation is accordingly become more complex, involving many decisions to be made in organising and using library services (cf. section 0).

- Libraries must develop strategies which help to reduce complexity for users; a important point of departure for these strategies is *integration* of resources and search tools, in order to provide a unified access point to networked information (cf. section 0).

- The traditional function of acquisition in libraries has to be expanded to a wider concept which we call *pre-selection*; this concept includes both acquiring electronic documents for local storage and creating links to selected resources on the external networks. Pre-selection is an appropriate method for enhancing availability and maintaining quality control over the content (and, if required, the language) of resources.

- Networked services pose serious problems with respect to the quality of information content and the quality of network access. Although many aspects of quality are outside the control of libraries, various options exist for enhancing the quality of the service provided (cf. section 0).

- The predominantly English-language nature of networked resources is a significant problem in the European context. An increase of materials in other language and the development of technical solutions will help to reduce this problem in the long run. In the short term, however, the problem remains; therefore librarians working in the field of networked information will have to acquire a certain level of proficiency in English. Careful pre-selection of resources based on language can help to isolate users from materials in languages they do not understand (cf. section 0).

- In the network environment, bibliographic control cannot be confined to documents, but has to be expanded to cover the description of information resources. This is a much wider concept, including any object (document, service, tool, organisation etc.) which can lead users to the knowledge they require. Taking into account the need for integration of access to networked resources, this eventually leads to a new type of integrated library >catalogue= (cf. section 0).

- Bibliographic description of networked resources requires adaptation of existing cataloguing rules, formats and systems. Descriptive cataloguing of networked resources is often problematic due to the lack of formal characteristics. A solution will in the future be found with the development of standardised >universal resource characteristics'. Accommodating access data in the bibliographic record is a difficult issue, currently solved redefining components of existing bibliographic formats such as USMarc field 856. In general, there is a need for a new generation of bibliographic systems which can handle the specific requirements of integrated access to networked information.

- Networked library services and the use of networked resources are relatively new phenomena with which most users are not familiar. There is therefore a special need for enhanced user support in this area. Libraries should develop a comprehensive range of support methods and make them available at various points in the knowledge mediation process. In view of the lack of experience in this area, it is important that libraries periodically review the need for support of their users. There is also a need for sharing experience and know-how in this area amongst libraries (cf. section 0).

- The future of networked library services will also include co-operation with publishers to provide networked distribution of and remote access to electronic versions of traditional publishing forms such as academic journals (cf. section 0).

- Reduction of complexity and integration of resources and tools, pre-selection and quality control, bibliographic control, and user support are important areas where the library can provide added value to users; they are the library's competitive assets in their competition with other service providers.

- Knowledge mediation using networked library services is a new and expanding area which as yet lacks a body of experience. Libraries constitute a controlled environment where the use of networked resources can be monitored, problems identified and new solutions created. It is important that librarians develop methods for sharing and communicating their experience and know-how.

The analysis provided in this part of the report can be used by libraries to plan the introduction of networked services as follows:

- The analysis of knowledge mediation concepts presented in sections 0 and 0 and in Appendix 2 provides the basic terminology for discussing the issues involved in networked library services. It is recommended that the library describes its current and future organisation using the structured list of concepts.

- Section 0, and also Figure 11 can be used to plan decision making and subsequent implementation for a number of important aspects of knowledge mediation in the networked environment. This document provides further material on a number of these issues:

  - Strategies for reducing complexity and integrating resource discovery can be developed based on suggestions given in section 0.

  - Guidelines for quality standards and control and language issues should be developed. Suggestions in this area are given in sections 0 and 0.

  - In the area of bibliographic control, guidelines for cataloguing networked resources should be established, preferably in co-operation with other libraries or based on emerging standards. Decisions need to be made on how to include networked resources in existing library systems, or to develop or acquire new systems in view of the increasing importance of networks (cf. section 0).

- It is essential that the library develops a comprehensive strategy for supporting the user in the networked environment. Suggestions in this area are given in section 0.

PART 3: APPLICATION MODELS

15. Application models for networked library services

In the previous part of this study (Analysis) we have identified a number of important issues for moving towards networked library services. In this part we translate the findings of the analysis into a number of scenario's or 'application models'. These models demonstrate how libraries can apply the concepts from the analysis to achieve appropriate levels of networked services for their users, taking into account different backgrounds of libraries.

15.1 Background factors

Before discussing models for application of networked library services, it is important to understand a number of factors which tend to be specific for individual libraries or groups of libraries, and which influence the way these libraries can or should proceed towards networked services.

15.1.1 Development stage and technical environment

What the library can and should to in developing towards networked library services depends to a high degree on its current use of information technology. Important factors are:

- The level of library automation and the systems used. Many library systems are not 'state-of-the-art' in a technical sense, and are not sufficiently based on open architectures to evolve easily towards the kind of functional integration described in Part 2 of this study.
- In addition to automated library systems as such, the availability of an internal network, servers, distributed processing power etc. are of course important.
- An all-important factor is the availability of a link to the global network infrastructure (in practical terms the Internet). If such a link is not available, the possibilities of networked services are extremely limited[22].
- The nature of the link is another decisive factor. The ideal situation is a dedicated link to the global network of sufficient capacity to cater for a large number of

---

[22]   It is, of course, possible to acquire networked resources from internal sources or other libraries (e.g. on diskette) or to download resources using a single dial-up network connection (e.g. from an Internet service provider) and to store them in a local system in the library. In that case however, active links to the network contained in such resources (e.g. WWW hypertext links) cannot be followed by the user.

simultaneous users. Many academic libraries can use the network connection provided by the parent institution. If a dedicated link is not available, the only alternative is to use a dial-up access provider. The cost of a dial-up link prohibits continuous use, especially for a larger number of concurrent users. In that case the library can only offer limited (possibly mediated) access 'on demand', in the same way as dial-up access to on-line databases.[23]

- An important aspect of networked library services is interlibrary co-operation. Activities in this area presuppose either communication through the Internet, or the use of a dedicated, co-operative library network.

- The development of networked library services is greatly enhanced if facilities are available at a centralised or national level. Such facilities are therefore to be regarded as a component of the library's 'technical environment'. An example is the Netherlands where a whole range of co-operative library services (including shared cataloguing, union catalogue, interlibrary lending, document delivery, on-line contents of journal articles, document servers and Internet cataloguing) are available through a well-organised national infrastructure developed by PICA and SURFnet. (cf. also section 0)

- Another variable which influences the development towards networked library services is the library user. Much depends on the user's skills in and attitudes towards using information technology and networks, and the technical resources to which they have access.

-

15.1.2 User awareness and expectations

Many library users, especially in the academic and business communities, are rapidly becoming familiar with networks as a communications and knowledge resource. Their expectations with regard to what networks can offer, are often far-reaching an simplistic. Many users expect that all knowledge resources soon will be available through the networks, and at low cost. This view is often shared by the library's fund providers.

---

[23]   Recently a number of CD-ROMs have been published which contain a collection of electronic resources (mostly downloaded from the Internet) in a specific domain. If the user can access the CD-ROM on his pc (via an internal or locally networked CD-ROM drive) with a network browser, the embedded links which are not on the CD-ROM can be accessed through the network). This is a cost-effective way to provide access to frequently used materials. Such CD-ROMs can ,of course, also be used by libraries without an active Internet connection, but in that case links to resources not contained on the CD-ROM cannot be accessed.

For many libraries, increasing user expectations with regard to electronic and networked services create a tension between what users demand and what the library can offer, given the available resources and circumstances. When the library cannot meet user expectations there is a serious possibility that users will access networked knowledge resources directly if they have an opportunity to do so. This creates an unfavourable situation for both sides: the user has to cope without the support and quality mechanisms of the modern networked library, and the library loses part of its user base. There is even a danger that negative experiences of users with networked resources adversely influence future activities of the library in this area.

It is therefore recommended that libraries carefully monitor user expectations, make the potential benefits of networked library services known to their users, and attempt to form an alliance with user groups, e.g. to divert resources targeted at individual users towards the library.

On the other hand, libraries should take care not to move too fast in offering 'hi-tech' services if their users are not sufficiently prepared. Although some users have high expectations and are very knowledgeable about new technologies, most users are tend to be conservative and do not like to change their information habits. Users need guidance in adapting to change, and need to be convinced of the added value of new services.

It should also be noted that networking has more to offer to users in some domains than in others. Computing is well presented on the network and in electronic documents, whereas musicology is much less so. Although the usefulness of networked services is increasing in almost all domains, the library should take care to chose the 'entry time' in such a way that users are not disappointed with what networked services can offer.

In summary, libraries should follow the following guidelines with regard to user satisfaction:

- Carefully monitor user expectations and changes in behaviour patterns.
- Provide adequate information to users and fund providers in order to create realistic expectations with regard to available resources, the cost involved, and the level of service the library can provide in the shorter term.
- Develop realistic plans for the development of networked services and form alliances with users in the process of obtaining funding.

- Take care to provide services which the users understand and are capable of becoming accustomed to without too much effort.
- Do not introduce networked services until sufficient networked knowledge resources are available for the domain covered by the library.

15.1.3 Staff awareness and skills

Introducing networked library services has consequences at all levels and for all functions of the library. In many instances developments towards new applications of information technology are initiated by a small group within the library who share a high level of knowledge and enthusiasm. Such a group can easily become isolated within the organisation, and fail to spread their knowledge, skills and excitement to the entire library staff. There is also a danger that the 'initiators' develop too high expectations (e.g. for services the library cannot afford), which eventually leads to disappointment and a decreasing level of involvement. These issues call for careful management, awareness building and staff training.

15.1.4 Financial resources

Migrating from a traditional library based on printed publications and stand-alone off-line electronic media to a fully networked environment has significant financial consequences for the library requiring additional financial resources. Although in the long run the use of electronic networked resources (and the implied opportunities for resource sharing) and servicing users over the network could lead to reductions in the operational cost of the library, a significant investment in new systems, staff training and organisational changes will be necessary. The available financial resources, and the success of the library in obtaining these resources are therefore a key factor for the move towards networked library services.

This being said, it is also true that providing at least a basic level of networked access in the library need not be extensive, provided there is at least a link to the Internet (cf. section 0). Many librarians are very inventive in providing new and interesting services using well-established and cheap technology. Even a stand-alone PC with an Internet browser will bring networked information into the library. Careful management of Bookmark lists (for which public domain software now exists) can help to present the user with a structured view of networked resources. However, it is clear that this is along way off from the concept of a fully networked library as described in this study.

An important question is how new library services should be funded, e.g. through central funding or by charging to users. This is a policy issue, and many libraries feel that they should be fully funded for their operations and that service should be free of charge to users. Their argument is that the cost of information services should be shared by all users, and that the best way to do this is through centralised funding by the community (for public libraries) or by the parent organisation (for academic and business libraries). However, there is a tendency in some circles to argue that whereas basic services should be free, the cost of added value services beyond these basic services could be recovered from those users who benefit specifically from the added value. Another argument is that charging to users leads to a better understanding of the cost and value of information, and to an increase in cost effectiveness. This argument is already being applied to many business libraries, which now operate as 'cost centres'.

The problem of choosing an appropriate funding method is complicated by the fact that in the field of electronic information the payment method is moving from subscriptions to access and 'pay-per-view' charging. Another development is site licensing, which covers certain types of access and under a flat fee, but also leads to additional charging on a per access basis for any other type of use. These developments result in problems of budgetary control for the library: an up-front payment (such as a subscription or license fee) is easy to manage, whereas payments based on type and volume of use are much less so. On the other hand, these developments offer more opportunities for charging to users, since the cost of use is more easy to monitor and calculate. In any case, networks also give access (either through the library or directly) to an increasing number of resources for which payment is required by the user accessing it. The 'networked payment mechanisms' now under development will certainly lead to an increase of services for which 'pay per use' by the user is required. It may even prove difficult for libraries to develop mechanisms which allow them to take on such charges, rather than the user.

To summarise, developing fully networked library services will carry significant development costs, and libraries should think carefully about ways to cover these. Charging to users for added value services is an option, and libraries should develop a policy in this area.

Two additional recommendations can be made here:

• Try to obtain a clear understanding of the way technology is developing and the extent to which prices may fall. Keep in mind that the latest in technology is usually the most expensive. On the other hand, take care to use technology with a development potential based on open standards.

- Investments in pilot projects should be based on a clear understanding of the financial implications of creating and maintaining an operational service after the pilot. Both the costs of upscaling (e.g. more and more powerful equipment) and operating (e.g. staff, servicing, training, copyright fees, etc.) have to be taken into account.

15.2 An approach to application models

The application models we discuss in this final part of the report are meant to describe the various components and functions of libraries which integrate traditional functions with networked services. They are meant to assist libraries to develop a future profile for their own operations in this area, and to set out a development path towards that model. These models are not meant to be descriptions of 'digital' libraries which concentrate on electronic resources. The challenge is to incorporate networked services and electronic resources with traditional, printed resources and on-site library use.

Libraries differ enormously in type (e.g. public, academic, government, business), development stage, technical environment, financial means, user community and even ambition. Given this wide disparity within the library sector, it is difficult to develop application models which describe networked services for each and every situation. The approach we take is to describe a number of generic models based on full use of current network technology and networked services. We then discuss ways for libraries to move towards these models.

In the following section we describe three basic models. The first of these is aimed at the individual library offering the highest level of integrated networked services. The second model describes distributing networked functions between libraries and 'national' or 'centralised' functions. Our third model looks at the library as a public information area which allows for a large variety of information-related activities for different user groups. Whereas the first two models are described in terms of functions, systems and processes, the third model is described in terms of the 'information environment', i.e. the things a user would encounter when visiting the library. These three models are not mutually exclusive. Rather, they describe various views of the networked library which we expect to emerge over the years.

16. The Networked Library model

In this model we describe the fully networked library which aims at utilising all network technologies and resources that are available today. It has to be stressed that this is an 'ideal' model, which describes a situation which does not yet exist, and which will be difficult to achieve for many libraries, at least in the short term. Nevertheless, by describing such an ideal (and perhaps idealistic) situation, it becomes clear what optimal application of networking can add to library services, and what is required to achieve that. The usefulness of the model is that it can be used by libraries to set their own specific objectives and put them in the context of an ideal situation.

The model described here is also an 'autarchic' model of an independent, self-sufficient library which has all the functions to provide full networked services to its users without having to rely on services provided by other libraries or library organisations. In the second model (cf. section 0) we describe co-operative approaches in which functions are shared amongst libraries, e.g. within the national context.

16.1 Components of the networked library system

In this model we view the library as an integrated networked system linked to the global network infrastructure (cf. Figure 12). According to this model, the library consists of the following components:[24]

- Storage facilities for electronic resources, consisting of:

  - One or more document servers on which individual documents are stored in electronic form and from which they can be downloaded to the user or sent to a printer.
  - One or more media servers for CD-ROMs, CD-Is etc. In general these media require a certain degree of user interaction, and may contain their own interfaces, search mechanisms, etc.
  - One or more database servers for structured sets of data and documents. These servers will include database management software which allows for user interaction and information retrieval.

---

[24] These components are discussed in more detail further on. It is taken for granted that the library will also have traditional components such as a storage area for printed resources, reading rooms etc.

- An integrated resource discovery system ('catalogue') which describes both internal and external resources.

- A support system which provides users with any type of (human or computer-mediated) assistance required.

- User workstations through which users can access the catalogue and internal and external resources as well as the support system.

- An administrative system, including functions for copyright management. The administrative system handles all 'technical' functions such as user registration, acquisitions, cataloguing, lending and document delivery, finance, etc.

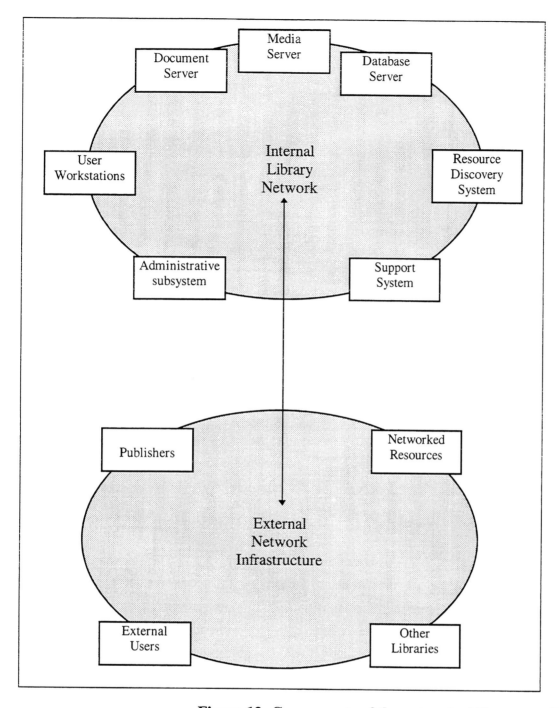

Figure 12: Components of the networked library model

The library is also connected to the 'external' network or global network infrastructure which, in terms of our model, contains the following components:

- Networked resources, i.e. the information services, systems and documents available on the global network infrastructure.

- Publishers and other resource suppliers who deliver resources (and accompanying bibliographic materials) through the network to the library.

- Other libraries with which the library maintains a relationship for providing services over the network (e.g. for document delivery).

- End users who access the library over the network ('remote users').

A further discussion of the networked library system components can be found in section 0.

16.2 The user's view of the library

For the user, the entry point to the library is through a user-oriented system which offers two distinct types of services:

- Knowledge mediation: functions which allow the user to identify, locate and obtain knowledge resources. The knowledge mediation service provides the user with a view on available knowledge resources and the means to acquire them.

- User support: functions which assist the user in using knowledge mediation functions. The user support system provides the user with a view on the library itself, the way it is organised, how to use functions and systems, the rules that have to be adhered to, etc.

These two basic functions are highly interrelated, i.e. at any point in the knowledge mediation process the user can switch to the support system, and vice versa. Context is built into the knowledge mediation system and supplied automatically. In other words: although the support system is always be available, it is only required in special cases (e.g. for learning how to use the system or for solving specific problems). The entire library system is conceived as a system to help the user find relevant information resources.

The way the knowledge mediation service is organised, will differ from library to library. In general it will consist of the following steps:

- A choice between locating known items or using a resource discovery system to identify unknown items.

- In the latter case: a choice between different subject domains, resource types (e.g. books, journals, networked resources), navigation tools (e.g. databases, library catalogues, network browsers), subject approaches (e.g. classification, thesaurus, full-text keywords), etc.

- A choice between alternative sources, formats and delivery methods.

In most libraries the available knowledge resources will include both electronic resources (stored on media and document servers) and printed resources. In principle, all resources *referred to* in the library's resource discovery system can be obtained by the user automatically, either in electronic form over the network or in printed form on-site, by fax or mail.

When a non-electronic resource is located through the knowledge mediation system, the library can choose to offer various levels of service:

- Require the user to request the document from the library desk
- Allow the user to access the printed resource from the library shelves
- Allow the user to send a request electronically to the library desk and obtain the document for consultation, loan or photocopying.
- Allow the user to send a request electronically for subsequent document delivery (e.g. by mail, fax or e-mail to the user's address). In the fully networked library this is the preferred option, and the only alternative for remote users.

16.3 Networked library functions

16.3.1 Acquisition

In the traditional library, acquisition policy relates to the documents that are acquired physically and stored and made available in the library. In the networked library, the concept of acquisition has a wider meaning. It pertains to the entire range of resources (including specific documents, but also document sources and services, e.g. FTP and Gopher sites, WWW home pages, search services etc.) which are made available to the user through the library's resource discovery mechanism(s), ideally the integrated resource catalogue. In other words: acquisitions policy defines the 'window' on available knowledge resources that the library wishes to present to its users. In view of the rapid changes in the world of networked information there is a need for frequent revision of acquisitions policy.

It has to be repeated here that the networked library described in this model is not a *digital* library. It includes both printed and electronic resources, and offers access to both internal resources (held by the library) and external resources (stored on the network). Acquisition comprises all these dimensions. The digital library can focus on networked electronic resources, and can focus on remote access (over the network) for its users. The networked library expands its knowledge mediating role to include, but not limit to electronic resources and networked access. This sense of integration, and the understanding that non-electronic and non-networked resources remain of importance, permeates the philosophy of the networked library and should therefore also be reflected in its acquisitions policy.

Acquisitions policy should also be based on a clear understanding of user needs, and user involvement at this stage is recommended.

Based on its acquisitions policy, the library should develop procedures for selecting and acquiring knowledge resources. Selection of printed resources is normally based on (secondary) information such as publisher catalogues, press announcements, bibliographies etc., and on requests and feedback from users. These sources remain valid in the context of networked resources, but will also include announcements on the network itself (e.g. mailed to listservers). However, a more important input to the selection process is a pro-active discovery approach (network monitoring) by the library itself, aimed at identifying relevant resources as they appear on the network. This requires specific knowledge, experience and skills which the library will have to

---

develop. There are an increasing number of network sites which systematically collect (links to) networked resources in specific domains; these can be used as pre-selection sources for acquisition.

As indicated above, acquisition pertains not only to the decision to 'acquire' a resource in terms of making it available. It also involves a number of additional decisions, e.g.:

- The decision to acquire the resource for local storage, or to provide only a link to its original (or possibly an archival) storage location on the network.
- The medium on which a resource is to be acquired (e.g. on CD-ROM or as a networked electronic document), if alternatives are available.
- The format in which the resource is acquired, if alternatives are available, and/or the format to which it is converted for storage and use.

Whereas traditional acquisition decisions are mainly based on intrinsic aspects of the resource such as subject matter, language, cost, quality etc., these additional decisions are much more related to user aspects such as type and frequency of use, available tools (e.g. at the user's desktop) etc. Other aspects are also important, e.g. resource format (highly fragmented HTML-resources are difficult to download) and update frequency (frequently updated, dynamic resources should not be stored locally).

Although the decision to acquire a resource for physical storage or to provide only a link to its network location is sometimes dictated by the nature of the resource, as mentioned above. Highly fragmented and dynamic resources, and resources which are services rather than documents, cannot effectively be stored locally. However, since this model is aimed at providing a uniform, integrated window to knowledge models based on pre-selection by the library, it makes sense to choose for local storage in most other cases. By doing so, the library can guarantee availability, ensure that documents are available in the right formats, and provide adequate and consistent cataloguing. In other words, the strategy is to rely more on 'real' acquisition and local storage, than on referring the user to other network sites, catalogues, search mechanisms etc.

In the networked library, acquisition and collection maintenance are highly interrelated. Decisions to remove an item from digital storage (and possibly to replace it by a link to an archival site on the network) will be taken frequently for many types of resources.

In the acquisitions process, electronic delivery by publishers to libraries is becoming an important issue. This issue is discussed in more detail under 'Publisher relations' below (section 0).

16.3.2 Resource storage

In the networked library, an increasing volume of knowledge resources is stored in electronic form. Three types of storage systems are available for these resources:

- *Media servers* for accessing off-line media such as DC-ROMs
- *Document servers* for accessing electronic documents stored individually on a file system.
- *Database servers* for accessing records or other information items stored within a database management system, normally including a separate retrieval mechanism.

Access to resources stored on these three types of servers will generally be through the library's resource discovery system or catalogue. There are, however, some distinctions to be made:

- Access to media servers through the resource discovery system is generally at the level of distinct media titles (e.g. a specific CD-ROM). The user will then be 'switched through' to the networked media server in order to access the title (and often, e.g. in the case of databases on CD-ROM, access further information through the media's embedded search interface). Media servers can also be accessed directly in stand-alone mode or over the internal network.

- Access to document servers through the resource discovery system results in a presentation of the requested document on the user's browser screen (e.g. similar to using a WWW browser), in a print-out or in downloading the document to the user's workstation. Depending on the type of material and possible license restrictions, the document server is also accessible directly over the (external) network, e.g. when implemented as an FTP or WWW server.

- Access to a database server through the resource discovery system normally either results in presentation of the requested record (if the discovery system identifies individual records) or in switching the user through to the server's database software (if the discovery system only identifies individual databases). If the database server contains unrestricted (e.g. non-copyright) materials, it is also made accessible over the external network, either via telnet or (preferably) using a Z39.50 interface.

Special consideration has to be given to *resource maintenance* and the preservation of electronic resources[25]. Two issues are important in this respect:

- *Media deterioration:* the life-expectancy of magnetic and optical storage media is limited (ranging from a few years for diskettes to 100 years for very high quality optical disks). The solution for media preservation is to periodically 'refresh' the information by transferring it to a new storage medium.

- *Technological obsolescence:* electronic information products are always based on a given 'technical environment' consisting of the hardware and software used for storing and accessing the information, the standards used for structuring and formatting the information, etc. When the technical environment changes (i.e. when new systems and standards are adopted), information based on the old environment becomes inaccessible. The solutions here are *migration* to the new technical environment (involving costly conversions procedures), or *emulation* of the old environment in the new one.

Careful planning and budgeting of resource maintenance is required. This has to be related to the library's retention policy, i.e. the extent to which the library wishes to store materials only for a short period in which frequent use is expected, or preserve them for a longer period as a 'historical' collection. Although the floor-space requirements of electronic materials are low, long-term preservation costs are expected to be significantly higher than those of printed materials, especially if migration to new technical environments is required.

16.3.3 Cataloguing

An important aspect of the value added by libraries to networked services is the creation of descriptive information or metadata ('bibliographic records') for networked resources. Describing resources in a consistent way (e.g. based on cataloguing rules), and specific bibliographic enhancements such as standardisation of names, addition of

---

[25]   The issue of resource maintenance cannot be covered fully in the context of this study. The issue is discussed in more detail in: Mackenzie Owen, J.S. ; Walle, J. v.d. - Study of issues faced by national libraries in the field of deposit collections of electronic publications. This is a study carried out by NBBI for the European Commission; the final report will be published by the Commission in the course of 1996.

subject identifiers, etc. greatly enhance the knowledge mediation process. It is precisely the lack of adequate resource description in carefully designed catalogues that is experienced as a problem by many current users of networked resources.

Cataloguing of networked resources (whether stored locally or available through links to the external network) can be effectively based on existing cataloguing rules with some expansions. These expansions are necessary to include data elements for specific characteristics of electronic publications, e.g.:

- resource type, e.g. document, database, library catalogue, search service etc.
- medium and data format
- access data for accessing the resource on the internal and/or external network
- access conditions, e.g. restricted access for registered users, fee-based, etc.
- version information and date/time stamps[26]

For original cataloguing of electronic resources by the library, a number of specific sources of descriptive data can be identified, e.g.:

- embedded metadata included in the publication
- the initial screen ('title screen') of the resource
- descriptive information on the previous access node (often the original link to a document is on a WWW page or Gopher menu containing descriptive information)
- accompanying materials in electronic form (e.g. 'read-me' files)
- other accompanying materials (e.g. packaging and manuals for CD-ROMs)

It is important to make a distinction in the bibliographic data between data required for automatic linking to network locations and data for presentation to the user. There is a need to develop specific data models for networked resources for the bibliographic system used by the library.

Cataloguing networked resources on an individual basis is of course an expensive and relatively inefficient activity. There are two developments in this area which will in future make the task easier:

- Shared cataloguing: there is already a move towards developing shared cataloguing on a national or domain basis. This means that in future libraries will be able to

---

[26] In the dynamic networked environment the concept of 'publication date' expressed as a year is inadequate. It is necessary to record the precise date and time of the instance of the document acquired.

obtain cataloguing data for networked resources from centralised sources. This issue is discussed in more detail in section 0.

- Cataloguing in publication: it is expected that in future most electronic documents will contain 'embedded metadata', i.e. descriptive information in a standardised format. This data can be used to create catalogue records automatically, to which local data (local network location, access conditions, subject identifiers) can be added.

16.3.4 Resource discovery

In the fully developed networked library the catalogue is a resource discovery system through which the library provides its window on knowledge resources to the user.

For the user, the resource discovery system is the access point to resources within the library and to resources available on the external network. This requires an expanded concept of the library catalogue as a repository of resource descriptions linked to internal and external sources of information (cf section 9 of the Conceptual Analysis). It should ideally provide access to all knowledge resources which the library wishes to make available to its users. This includes both printed and electronic resources, both documents and other resources types (external catalogues, databases, search mechanisms, document sites, WWW pages, Gopher menus etc.), both within and outside the library.

In developing the library's resource discovery system, it is useful to view the catalogue not as a system which links requests to documents, but as a device which provides intelligent answers to user requests. This concept is useful to convey the idea of the 'expanded' catalogue providing access to *resources* which are not necessarily documents. Examples of the types of such responses are:

- These are documents which seem to satisfy your request. You can find them at the indicated locations in the library.
- These are documents which seem to satisfy your request. You can view/download/print them now if you wish.
- We do not have any suitable resources in this library. We are now passing you on to another library which we believe can help you. There is no need to repeat your request since we have passed it on automatically.

- We do not have any suitable resources in this library. We suggest you contact the following persons/organisations which are specialised in your field.
- We are not able to find any resources which satisfy your request. Please contact the library staff who can help you further.
- We are not able to find any resources which satisfy your request. We have therefore passed you on the our on-line help desk. My name is John...

Creating and maintaining such a resource discovery requires not only changes to the existing library system in a technical sense. It also, and especially, requires careful thinking about the structuring of (references to) resources, about problems of indexing and classification, and about developing new search mechanisms within the catalogue. Traditional author/title and subject searches need to be expanded to search methods for resource and media types, intellectual quality, cost etc. It also requires, of course, the training of library staff to clearly understand and handle the expanded concept of cataloguing and metadata in the networked environment.

The networked library will provide a 'window' on knowledge resources which is of the highest quality and which solves the many insufficiencies of existing search mechanisms on the Internet. If this can be achieved, the library will be able to provide added value and retain an important role as a knowledge mediator. In addition to the quality of the resources to which the library provides access and the level of user support it provides, the quality of its internal search mechanism or 'resource catalogue' will be its 'unique selling point' in relation to other information service provides on the network.

Special consideration has to be given to the relationship between the library's own resource discovery system and that of other libraries to which the library may refer. These could be traditional library catalogues accessible via telnet, full resource discovery systems as described here, or anything in between. Given that it would not seem possible at the present moment to arrive at the concept of a 'global distributed library catalogue' which would appear to the user as a single catalogue of all libraries in the world[27], the ideal situation should at least have the following characteristics:

---

[27] Interesting developments in this direction are however already taking place. In the Netherlands, for instance, the on-line union catalogue of Dutch libraries is being expanded to include networked resources and links from metadata to document sources. Eventually this will develop into an integrated resource discovery system covering all materials available in libraries in the Netherlands. However, this is also a move towards the co-operative model described in section 17).

- References to other library catalogues and databases are included in the resource discovery system. Descriptive data is attached in such a way that subject oriented requests are resolved by a link to a library which is expected to contain the type of materials requested. In other words, the response to a request which cannot be resolved through the library's own resources, is responded to by switching the library to another catalogue or database where the system thinks it can be resolved.

- When switching the user to another library catalogue or database, the user's original request is passed on to the new resource discovery system and processed automatically.

- The user interface of another library catalogue or database is identical to that of the user's own library (e.g. based on Z39.50).

16.3.5 User access

An important characteristic of the fully networked library is the fact that it provides various levels of access to its user: on-site access, remote access over the network, and document delivery. As already mentioned, the real challenge for libraries is to provide both on-site and remote access in a way which integrates printed and electronic, internal and external resources, and offers its users an added value in comparison with organisations which provide only networked access to information or document delivery services.

- *On-site access.* The networked library remains a place which users can visit as a well-organised information environment[28]. In spite of the attractiveness of access to information in the work place or at home, the library as a physical location continues to offer a number of advantages:

  - The library can offer the most sophisticated and up-to-date tools for identifying and obtaining information, and can do so for users who are not in a position to obtain such access themselves.

  - The library offers immediate access to non-electronic resources and to off-line electronic resources such as CD-ROMs.

---

[28]   Cf. also section 18: The Knowledge Environment Model

- The library is a human environment where personal assistance can be obtained, and where there is an opportunity to meet and converse with other people. Such a 'social environment' remains attractive to many users.

It should be noted that the networked library is expected to offer sufficient 'electronic workplaces' (e.g. networked workstations), printing and downloading facilities etc. to cope with the expected volume of on-site users.

Providing integrated on-site access to printed and electronic, internal and external resources is the main challenge for libraries wishing to maintain the traditional function of the library, whilst expanding it with networked services.

It is needless to say that on-site access also includes 'traditional' lending of resources (mainly printed documents, but also off-line media such as educational software on diskettes and possibly CD-ROMs) to users and the opportunity to make photocopies, print-outs and copies on off-line media (e.g. diskettes) in as far as there are no legal restrictions.

- *Remote access.* In the networked environment, it is inevitable that many users will require remote access to the library over the network. The networked library is therefore also a 'virtual' library which can be used to its full extent over the network. The concept of 'virtual reality' is especially appropriate here, since remote access implies not only access to the library catalogue (or resource discovery system) or to individual functions. It is rather a re-creation of the library in an electronic networked context. Spatial representation, perhaps in 3D virtual reality mode, is necessary to help the user to enter and find his way through the library. Developing full-scale remote access involves the following steps:

  - Developing the virtual environment for the remote user.
  - Developing adequate on-line support mechanisms
  - Ensuring that all resource discovery systems (including internally networked off-line systems such as databases on CD-ROMs) are accessible over the external network.
  - Coping with non-electronic materials.
  - Providing user authorisation and access control. This is especially important in view of the fact that the use of electronic materials often is governed by campus or site licenses which limit access to authorised users.

16.3.6 Document delivery.

Document delivery is not only a function of networked services where documents are delivered electronically to the user over the network. Networked document delivery is in fact implied by the concept of networked access, but only as far as electronic resources are concerned. Requests for delivery of non-electronic documents will have to be fulfilled by other means. In addition, both electronic and printed documents can be requested (e.g. by telephone, mail or e-mail) by external users (including other libraries) who have no access to the networked library system. Document delivery in the networked library includes the following functions:

- Delivery of electronic resources over the network as a direct result of the knowledge discovery process (e.g. by viewing or downloading an identified resource).

- Copying of printed resources and off-line printing of digital resources in the library and subsequent delivery by mail or fax.

- Lending and delivery of printed resources and off-line media by mail.

- Digitisation of printed resources and delivery over the network.

- Delivery of materials (by any of the above-mentioned means) by other libraries through interlibrary lending or co-operative document delivery schemes.

Document delivery is a sensitive area, since it involves issues of copyright and 'fair use' of materials. Libraries should take care to monitor ongoing developments in this area. Increasingly, libraries will be forced to charge for document delivery services, not only to cover operational cost but especially to copyright fees payable under copyright rules. Libraries should also understand that different rules apply to digital storage and related services than to print. There is a tendency to require not only payment of copyright fees, but also explicit permission from the copyright holder for the type of digital storage on which electronic document delivery is based.

16.3.7 User support

User support is an essential component of the added value that libraries can offer in the networked environment. It is therefore a well-developed function which encompasses more than the availability of helpful staff in the library and a printed library guide[29].

---

[29]   The various functions and methods of user support have been elaborated in section 10 of the Conceptual Analysis and are not repeated here.

In the networked library, user support is offered at two levels: human support and computer-mediated support.

- Support by library staff is available on a face-to-face basis for on-site users. In addition, contact can be sought with support staff over the telephone, by e-mail and, especially for remote users, by means of an real-time, interactive conversation system (comparable to IRC on the Internet) which allows the on-line user to enter into communication with library staff over the network. The conversation system is available as a separate function when entering the 'virtual' library on-line, and also as a 'fallback' service from the resource discovery system.

- Computer-mediated assistance is available as an embedded support function of the library system. It is available both as a separate function, and as a context-sensitive help function in the resource discovery system. It comprises at least the following sub-functions:

  - A *visual floor-plan* of the library, directing the user to appropriate sections of the library. The floor-plan is 'intelligent, i.e. it can respond to questions from the user (e.g. 'Where can I...') by giving appropriate directions. The floor-plan is a component of the visual representation of the library for remote access.

  - A *library guide* which instructs the user how to perform specific actions in the knowledge discovery process. The library guide can respond to specific questions (e.g. 'How can I...') or be used as a structured tutorial. It is also embedded in a context-sensitive way in the resource discovery system, i.e. when the user runs into problems, he is referred to appropriate sections of the library guide.

  - *System guides* which describe the use of specific systems, tools etc. System tools are sub-components of the overall library guide. They are embedded as a context-sensitive help function in the library system. System manuals are essentially structured hypertext documents, similar to Windows Help-files, and including functions for topic searching, temporary bookmarks, printing or downloading of help-topics, etc.

16.4 Networked library systems

The networked library model ideally requires an entirely new approach to library systems. The basic components have already been described in section 0. A generic model of the library system is presented in Figure 13.

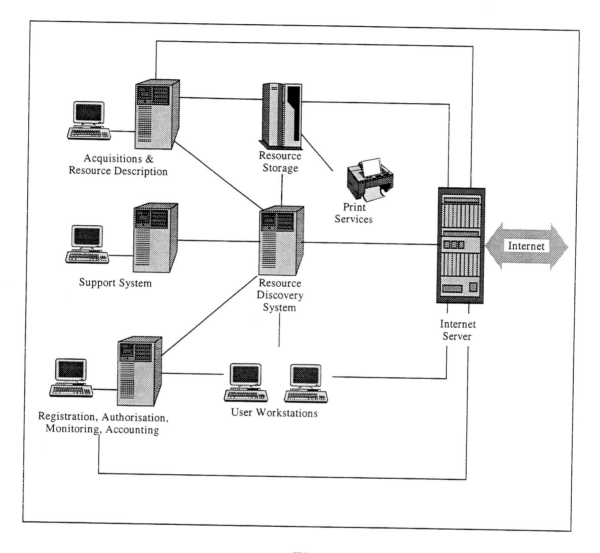

Figure 13: The networked library system

This model makes clear that there are two major differences between the networked library system and traditional library systems as used in most libraries today:

- The networked library system is an open, modular system based on the client/server architecture and an internal local area network infrastructure. It is based on open standards which allows linking to other open systems and easy integration of system modules. The network protocols are either based on ISO standards or (increasingly) on TCP/IP. The user interface is based on Internet-type browsers (where necessary enhanced by Java applets) and Z39.50/ISO10162/3. The various modules are linked, via the internal network, to an Internet server which handles all communications with the global network infrastructure. Access to the library system over the internally networked workstations or over the external Internet is entirely transparent to the user. In summary: the technology base of the networked library system is entirely different from that of many library systems currently in operation.

- The networked library system is based on a different, integrated approach to traditional library functions:

  - Acquisitions and cataloguing (or rather: resource description) are highly integrated for two reasons. First, acquisition encompasses not only the physical acquisition of resources, but also the process of selecting and making available resources which are not held locally in the library, but are made accessible over the external network. Second, descriptive data for networked resources will in future normally be obtained over the network together with the resources themselves, either as separate datasets or as metadata embedded in the resources. It should be noted that this module also handles standard technical services such as acquisitions and cataloguing of non-electronic resources.

  - Resource storage is a component of the library system, as described in section 0, and direct links exist between resource descriptions and their storage locations. Traditional library systems do not contain an integrated resource storage function.

  - The resource discovery system is based on an expanded concept of the library catalogue, as described in section 0. The support system, although conceived as a separate module, is tightly linked to the resource discovery system. As illustrated in the model, the resource discovery system is the key integrative component of the networked library system. It is through this module that the user accesses the library functions, retrieves resources, obtains support, and handles administrative transactions.

  - Registration, authorisation, monitoring and accounting (RAMA) is a module which handles all administrative relations between the library and its users. Although it handles traditional lending operations, its functionality is greatly expanded. For a variety of reasons, users of the networked library are normally registered. Access to library services such as document delivery normally require authorisation (e.g. based on passwords and perhaps a PIN-code), as does access to resources for which license restrictions apply and for materials and services that are charged to the user. Monitoring of library use is required for management purposes, and in many cases also to comply with license conditions. Accounting is required for 'pay-per-use' functions, handling payments to resource and service suppliers, and for end-user charging if appropriate.

Document delivery services are not indicated in section Figure 13.for reasons of clarity, but are of course an integrated function of the networked library system. They are a combination of the following sub-functions:

- Sending documents or photocopies to the user by mail or fax, possibly after printing from resource storage.
- Sending electronic resources to users by e-mail.
- Transmitting electronic resources to users from resource storage via FTP.

Another component which is not shown explicitly is the 'virtual' library model through which external users access the library over the network (cf. section 0). This is conceived of as a front-end interface to the resource discovery system.

The model described in Figure 13 is a generic model which gives an overall view of system components and their interconnection. In practical implementations, further modularisation will often be appropriate. For instance, resource storage could consist of separate resource servers (cf. section 0), and the registration, authorisation, monitoring and accounting functions could be implemented as separate, though tightly interrelated modules.

A number of interconnections between system components need explanation:

- As already mentioned, the resource discovery system is the key integrative module, and connected to all other modules.

- The acquisitions and resource description module provides input to resource storage (acquired electronic resources) and to the resource discovery system (resource descriptions).

- The support system is, as already mentioned, tightly linked to the resource discovery system.

- The link between the registration, authorisation, monitoring and accounting module and the resource discovery system allows for full control of user access and for recording relevant data with regard to access and use.

- User workstations are linked to the resource discovery system as the primary access point to the library's knowledge mediation service. There is also a link to the registration, authorisation, monitoring and accounting module to allow users to register with the library, change passwords and perform other administrative functions.

- The links to the external network infrastructure (normally the Internet) can be summarised as follows:

    - Acquisitions: a proportion of the electronic resources acquired by the library is received over the Internet.

    - Resource description: bibliographic data for resources stored in the library, and data on and links to external resources are received over the Internet. A link to the Internet is also required for maintenance of network locators (URLs) for resources linked to in the resource discovery system.

    - Resource storage can be accessed over the network directly as an FTP or WWW site. One or more printer servers are attached to the storage module for on-line and off-line printing.

    - The resource discovery system can be accessed over the Internet through an embedded 'virtual library model' front-end.

    - The support system is accessible over the network, either directly or as an embedded function of the resource discovery system (cf. section 0).

    - User workstations provide access not only to the internal library system and the range of knowledge resources available through the library's resource discovery system, but also to other resources on the global network infrastructure.

- The registration, authorisation, monitoring and accounting module is linked to the Internet for two reasons. First, this allows remote users to register with the library, change passwords and perform other administrative functions. Second, this link allows for electronic transactions (EDI) with publishers (ordering and payment) and with other libraries (e.g. ILL-request using the ISO 101160/1 interlibrary lending protocols).

16.5 Publisher relations

Looking at current developments in the world of publishing, it becomes clear that the 'traditional' distinction between printed and electronic publications is no longer adequate[30]. Electronic publications can be thought of to include off-line publications such as CD-ROM or CD-I (and other types such as educational software), and networked publications which can be accessed from a document server or WWW-site. What we are now seeing, is a move towards 'electronically distributed' publications. Publishers, especially in the field of scientific journals, are now beginning to distribute their traditional titles to libraries in electronic form. These are not electronic publications in the strict sense, but rather electronic *versions* of traditional, printed publications. In most cases, publishers also provide bibliographic data ('metadata') together with these electronic versions, which can be used to create catalogue entries. Libraries can store

The publisher is therefore becoming a source of electronic materials and of catalogue data. This development clearly influences not only the way in which the library has to handle its existing tiles (e.g. journals), but also changes the relationship between the library and the publisher. This relationship is reflected in the inclusion of *license agreements* which specify the conditions under which the materials are obtained. Most notably, they specify the level and type of access to the materials that the library is allowed to offer its users.

For instance, such agreements can put limits on the user group (e.g. only registered users or members of the parent organisation), the type of use (e.g. only view, print or download), the access mode (e.g. only on-site or over the internal network), and require special mechanisms for authorising and monitoring access, feedback of usage data, etc.

---

[30]   Cf. section 12, Networked relations with publishers.

In some cases the publisher can also require the library to subscribe to a printed copy of the publication before delivering the electronic version at an additional fee.

In other words, the library enters into specific, legal relationships with publishers which put the library under special obligations with respect to access and use, and which may require specific technical and organisational measures in order to assure compliance with license agreements. This is very different from the traditional situation where the library has no special relationship with publishers, and where use is governed by generic legal conditions such as copyright law.

- Purchasing printed publications from publishers, either directly or through booksellers and subscription agents.
- Purchasing off-line documents from publishers (possibly through an intermediary 'media seller').
- Providing access to commercial publications on the network, either on a 'pay per access' basis or in the context of a license agreement.
- Obtaining publications in electronic form from publishers, on a subscription basis and under a license agreement which specifies allowable use.

An additional remark to be made here, is that licensing agreements can offer the opportunity of more flexible budgeting. For instance, the library can agree to pay the publisher on a 'pay per access' basis, which means that the cost of materials which are used infrequently (but nevertheless need to be available in the library) are relatively lower than that of highly used resources. This approach also provides a good basis for charging users for certain types of materials which the library itself may not be able to afford.

17. The Co-operative Network model

The model of the fully networked library discussed in the previous section is based on the assumption that individual libraries will create their own collections of electronic resources, create bibliographic data for internal and external resources, provide their own document delivery services for end-users, etc. What is becoming clear, however, from recent developments in more advanced countries (in Europe notably the United Kingdom and the Netherlands) is that another approach is possible if there exists a co-operative library infrastructure. In our second model we describe how many of the networked library functions can be distributed amongst libraries or library organisations, in a way which makes more efficient use of resources on a national scale and which allows a larger number of libraries to offer networked services to their users.

17.1 A client-server approach

The idea behind this model is that networking allows libraries to share efforts by providing services to each others users. Under this model, it is useful to make a distinction between libraries which concentrate on serving their own users, and libraries which have a wider function in providing services to a (subsection) of the library community. Traditionally the latter group included libraries which operate on a national level, such as national libraries and (mostly academic) libraries which offer services to other libraries in a certain domain. Since national boundaries are becoming increasingly less important in the network environment, we prefer to adopt the 'client-server' metaphor for describing the relationship between these two types of libraries. Within this metaphor, 'server libraries' are libraries which offer services to other libraries, often on a national basis, within a certain domain or for a specific type of libraries. These other libraries are referred to as 'client libraries'. The metaphor is useful, since it includes the notion that the client-server relationship is based on close co-operation, a division of functionality, and the mutual acceptance of standards.

- *Server libraries* take on the task of developing fully networked services in a specific subject domain such as the social sciences, engineering or the arts, or as a national service covering all domains. They do this either as an extension to their traditional services (i.e. following the model outlined in section 0), or as an exclusively 'digital' library limited to electronic resources. Services offered by server libraries include a collection of electronic resources, a domain-oriented resource discovery system, document delivery services and domain-specific support.

- *Client libraries* do not to develop full-scale services in areas covered by domain-based or national server libraries. Instead, they act as an interface to these server libraries. Client libraries can either just switch users through to domain servers, or they can develop a close integration between their own services and those provided by other libraries.

It is important to note that a library can take on both roles simultaneously by acting as a server library in one domain, and interfacing as a client to server libraries in other domains.

17.2 Domain-based and national services

Although many variants are of course possible, two main approaches to the co-operative library network model are:

- The *domain-based approach* (Figure 14). In this approach libraries are assigned tasks on a domain basis. For each domain (such as medicine, social sciences, the arts, engineering) a single library develops a comprehensive 'electronic' service, including document servers, resource discovery mechanisms, etc. Other libraries connect their own users to one of these domain services when their request falls in the specified domain.

	DOMAIN-BASED APPROACH	
	Client library	**Server library (domain service)**
Resource description	No local cataloguing for server domains	Cataloguing of all resources accessed through server
Or:	Shared cataloguing effort as input to server's resource discovery system	Maintenance of shared cataloguing system based on input from client libraries and other sources.
Resource discovery	Umbrella interface to domain-based services + RDS for locally held printed and electronic resources	Full resource discovery system for national collection of resources.
Resource storage	Minimal local storage of networked resources	Substantial volume of local storage of networked resources + external resources
Or:	Storage distributed over client libraries	Limited central storage.
User support	General support	Specific support (e.g. for national resources)

Figure 14: The domain-based approach to co-operative library services

- The *national service approach* (Figure 15). This approach is more far-reaching, and perhaps only feasible in smaller countries. It implies that one (national) library (or library organisation), or a small number of co-operating libraries provide a national electronic service to which other libraries interconnect. The functions to be performed by such a national service are similar to those performed by domain-based services, but they cover the entire range of networked electronic resources (with the exception of off-line resources such as locally networked CD-ROMs).

NATIONAL SERVICE APPROACH		
	Client library	**Server library (national service)**
Resource description	No or limited local cataloguing of electronic resources	Centralised cataloguing of all resources accessed through server
Or:	Shared cataloguing effort as input to server's resource discovery system	Maintenance of shared cataloguing system based on input from client libraries and other sources.
Resource discovery	Umbrella interface to national service +RDS for locally held printed and electronic resources	Full resource discovery system for networked resources
Resource storage	Storage distributed **Or:** over local libraries	Storage on centralised national server
User support	General support	Specialised support

Figure 15: The national approach to co-operative library services

17.3 Integration at the client level

An important design consideration for the co-operative networked library is the level of integration offered to the user. Two specific models can be followed:

- The *switchboard model:* when the user enters the library's resource discovery space, he is immediately switched to a server library (either the user's own library or another library) which can handle the user's request. All further transactions are handled by the server library. This come down to a partitioning of the available resource space into discrete services. The main function of the resource discovery system of the client library is to assist the user in choosing an appropriate server. The user is aware of being switched to another library, and of having to use the server's interface, support system, etc. In a technical sense, this is of course not a true implementation of client-server principles.

- The *integration model:* a more sophisticated approach is to integrate the functionality of the server library with local functions at the client level. This means that the services offered by the server are perceived of by the user as being part of his own library's system. Such a seamlessly integrated, transparent requires full implementation of the client-server architecture over the distributed resource space.

17.4 Steps towards a co-operative network model

The client-server approach described the previous sections is not sufficient to arrive at a fully co-operative network, model. It also requires shared efforts in acquiring and storing networked resources, creating metadata, etc. In other words: a fully co-operative model should be based on co-operation in the creation and management of resources, as well as on shared use of resources. In developing towards such a co-operative network model the following steps can be taken:

- *Shared cataloguing of networked resources.* Under the shared cataloguing model, the participants in the co-operative network contribute resource descriptions to a central metadata repository. This is either used as the basis for a shared resource discovery system, or used as input to local resource discovery systems. Co-operative schemes for creating metadata for networked resources are under development in a number of countries, e.g. the Netherlands (CC-Internet) and the United States (OCLC Catalog of Internet Resources).

- *Resource sharing.* This implies agreements amongst libraries in a certain domain, or at the national level, to share the effort of collecting and storing networked resources. This is normally done by giving each library responsibility for a well-defined collection area. Usually each library will also be responsible for publications of the parent institution, government sector, region, etc. Resource sharing will normally imply some form of shared cataloguing as the basis for creating a shared, 'virtual' collection of electronic materials. An example of this is the WebDOC project in the Netherlands.

- *Creating a virtual library infrastructure.* Once resource sharing and shared cataloguing of electronic resources are in place, some further steps are necessary to arrive a virtual library infrastructure which is sufficiently transparent to appear to the user as a single networked library covering a specific domain or country. These steps are mainly concerned with developing the networked library functionality described in section 0. The main steps can be summarised as follows:

  - development of an integrated resource discovery system; the same system is preferably used by all libraries participating in the network;

- development of co-operative document delivery procedures;
- development of co-operative relationships (including license agreements) with publishers for the distribution of electronic versions of publications and accompanying metadata;
- development of appropriate user support procedures;

17.5 The need for local services

It is important to be aware of the fact that there is a problem with the distributed approaches described in this section. Individual libraries will have to cope with yet another level of integration. They do not only have to integrate printed and electronic resources, but also local and distributed services. It is not yet clear how this should be done and what kind of problems may arise. It could, however, mean that funding is directed more towards 'centralised' services, and that individual libraries find it more difficult to find funding for networking their own resources and systems.

Libraries may even lose their user base if users access domain-based or national services directly. It is however a misunderstanding to believe that with the distributed approach there is no need for the concept of 'local' libraries. Local libraries contain valuable resources which distributed electronic libraries cannot offer, e.g. their current stock of printed resources, off-line media (such as CD-ROMs), special collections etc. They can also adapt their 'knowledge window' to the specific needs of local users, and can provide specific forms of user support. The development of more centralised networked library services does not diminish the value of local libraries, but it does make it more difficult for them to defend their case.

18. The Knowledge Environment model

18.1 The public library as a knowledge environment

In developing the previous two models, the focus has been on the knowledge mediation *process* and its various functions. The knowledge discovery system is regarded as the key component. It functions as the mechanisms through which the library presents a selective window on available knowledge resources, and through which the user identifies and obtains or accesses these resources. As we have seen, this type of library depends very much on aspects such as increasing digitisation, network access, advanced man-machine interfaces, etc. This type of networked library, although existing in the real world, can be experienced by remote users as a 'virtual library' implemented on the network. It is aimed at sophisticated users, with high-level information needs and capable of using advanced technological means.

One should, however, regard the library is not only a 'knowledge mediation mechanism', but also as a 'knowledge environment', i.e. a physical place where people come - perhaps even without explicit information needs - to find, use and exchange information. This approach focuses more on a user-oriented perception of the library, i.e. on what the user will find and do in the library, rather than on the way the library's functions and systems are organised.

The model we use to illustrate this approach (Figure 16: The Networked Public Library) is based on the public library as an example where this approach seems more appropriate than the more academic library environment on which the previous models are based implicitly. However, the approach taken here, based on the concept of the library as a 'knowledge environment' or 'information space' where users can perform a wide variety of information-related activities, can of course be adapted to other types of libraries as well.

18.2 Characteristics of the public library

A number of special characteristics of the public library have to be taken into account:

- *The meaning of media.* For most academic users, the type of information medium is usually not very important, unless is has specific characteristics which are required to convey a certain type of message. For instance, information on new operating techniques could best be conveyed by using video. But in general, for academic users, the message is more important than the medium. While this is of course often also the case for users of public libraries, the medium itself is of specific importance for many users as well. For instance, some users enjoy browsing the Internet, watching videos or playing computer games. In general, younger generations can be attracted to the library by making it an exciting place, offering a mix of educational and recreational experiences. Multimedia and network technology offer ample opportunities for doing this.

- *The diversity of user expectations.* In the academic environment one can expect users to adapt to new facilities and tools fairly easily. Often, users will even expect a more sophisticated use of technology than the library is able to offer. In the public library, although some users will expect and appreciate a sophisticated, 'modern' technical environment in the library, many other users will not be willing to switch to networked resources and multimedia. Here, the library will have to continue offering its traditional services based on printed resources, physical lending and face-to-face user support.

- *The diversity of user skills.* Whereas in the academic environment users often obtain training in using the library and handling information, and gain continuous experience through their work, this is not the case with users of the public library. General 'information education' within the educational system varies from country to country, but will in general not be sufficient to allow users of the library to make optimal use of existing facilities and to adapt easily to new services. Special attention therefore has to be given to user instruction and user support, and to offering different types of instruction and support for different groups of users.

- *The social role of the library.* Most public libraries are far more than information providers or 'knowledge mediators'. The public library is also a social institution serving specific functions within its community. This role has to be taken aboard and developed further when adopting network technologies. More specifically, the networked public library will put special emphasis on community and citizenship information and on providing access to community information systems, digital cities, government information services, and home pages of social advisory organisations as the main networked resources of interest to the user.

- *The language issue.* For most public libraries, it is essential to make sure that networked resources in the library are in the national language (except of course materials in foreign languages for users who specifically wish to read these languages). The as yet problematic issues concerning the language of network tools and resources described in section 0 are especially important to the public library.

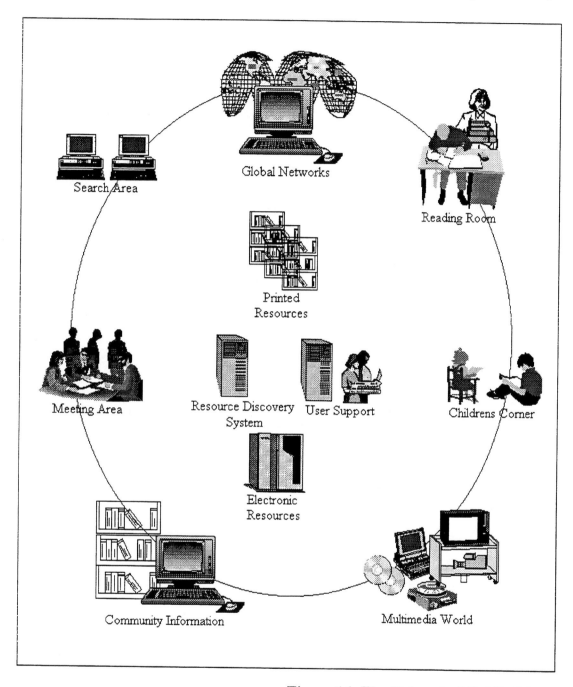

Figure 16: The Networked Public Library

18.3 The networked public library functions

In this model, the library consists of a number of functional areas which take into account the different types of users and user needs for which the public library has to perform its services. Examples of such functional areas are:

- The *Meeting Area*, close to the entrance of the library, is where people can meet and communicate informally. It is a public area, and not necessarily restricted to registered users. In larger places, it contains or is integrated with shops, a café or restaurant, perhaps even a cinema. The Meeting Area also offers public telephones and fax machines, and network terminals for sending e-mail. Registered users can also obtain an electronic mailbox for receiving e-mail.

- The library contains a *Search Area* (or 'Discovery Area') where the user can access the library's resource discovery system, and reference works in printed and multimedia form. This area is for the serious user who is in search of answers to a question or solutions to a problem; it also serves as an 'electronic reading room' for consulting electronic resources.

- *Global Networks* is the area where full, unmediated access to the global network infrastructure is offered. This area could be set up as an 'Internet cafeteria' where refreshments are available.

- Since the library also serves people who are not interested in using networks and multimedia, there is a quiet *Reading Room* for consulting printed materials. This an area where the atmosphere of the traditional library is best preserved.

- *Community Information* is an area for the socially or politically involved user. Here one can find answers to social issues, information related to the environment, etc. It is also possible to participate in political debate. Community Information is next to the meeting area, since it serves as a more specific meeting area, e.g. where citizens can discuss issues concerning their community, and where they can communicate with government agencies and politicians can communicate, either or over the network.

- *Multimedia World* contains a large variety of multimedia resources and equipment. Here users can watch television, listen to music recordings, play computer games, use recreational and educational multimedia or create their own multimedia programmes. Some multimedia resources and even equipment can be borrowed from the library. Multimedia World can be rather noisy, but there are also sound-isolated cubicles available.

- *Children's Corner* is next to Multimedia World, because children are one of the main users of multimedia. It is also a place where parents can leave their children safely while doing other things, and where members of the library's staff are allowed to read to their youngest users.

These user-oriented functions are, of course, supported in the background (i.e. more or less hidden from the user) by the library's internal network and links to the global network infrastructure, by systems components such as a resource discovery system, an automated user support system, digital storage, etc., and by traditional library functions such as acquisitions, cataloguing, lending and document delivery, etc.

18.4 Network aspects

In the networked public library, two aspects of networking are important.

- Internally, many electronic resources (perhaps with an emphasis on interactive multimedia) are used. The various tools and resources are interlinked over the internal network, and access to most resources is available from more than one area (e.g. community information directly in the Community Information area, or indirectly through the resource discovery system; the Internet directly from Global Networks or through the resource discovery system; multimedia reference works both in the Search Area and in Multimedia World).

- The library also maintains a number of external network links in a variety of ways:

  - Access to the global network infrastructure is provided in a pre-selective way through the library's resource discovery system, and on an unrestricted basis through direct access to the network, e.g. through WWW-browsers.
  - The (public) library serves as an access point to community and government information services.
  - Many functions (such as resource discovery, access to community information, document delivery) are available to remote users (possibly over existing cable-TV networks), e.g. citizens at home.

19. A development path towards networked library services

In the previous sections we have described a number of application models for networked libraries which illustrate what types of service they can offer when making full use of computer and network technology. In this section we present a schematic model of the development path from the current low level of application of network technology to the higher levels of application described in the application models.

The development path described here is structured according to the main library functions. For each function, an initial stage of development is described, followed by specific development steps towards an intermediate and a fully developed stage.

Since many libraries, especially in the less developed regions, will find it difficult to reach full levels of application in the short term, the levels described here under the initial and intermediate stage may well represent more realistic objectives in many cases.

	Initial stage	Intermediate stage	Developed stage
Acquisition	In the initial stage, acquisition will be based on printed publications and perhaps some off-line electronic publications such as CD-ROM and CD-I on stand-alone (non-networked) machines. the library may also have experience with on-line databases accessed by dial-up connections to host organisations.	More emphasis is given to acquiring off-line electronic resources which can be accessed from networked workstations. In addition, access to the Internet is provided through a dial-up connection in order to download networked resources, either for printing or for local storage..	Full access to external networked resources is provided through a dedicated link to the Internet. This includes access to on-line databases through the Internet. A certain amount of electronic resources is stored locally on dedicated servers. Local storage is preferred for resources produced locally (e.g. within the parent organisation) or for which long-term availability has to be guaranteed. The majority of knowledge

	Initial stage	Intermediate stage	Developed stage
			resources relevant to users are not stored locally, but are accessible over the network. Most materials are acquired in electronic form from publishers or directly from authors (e.g. within the parent organisation). The library has entered into resource sharing agreements with other libraries.

	Initial stage	Intermediate stage	Developed stage
Resource description	In the initial stage, cataloguing (based mainly on printed materials) is done manually and/or based on bibliographic data obtained through shared cataloguing systems (e.g. as provided by PICA, OCLC).	The library has developed catalogues or resource lists of networked resources, possibly with active links to network locations. It has also developed structured bookmark lists for Internet browsers, referring to selected networked resources, and it provides pointers to additional sources of bibliographic information (including directories, catalogues, networked bibliographies etc.), e.g. implemented as WWW-pages or browser bookmarks. Creating lists of and pointers to networked resources is regarded as a normal component of the cataloguing profession.	The library has developed an integrated resources discovery system which describes all available resource data types and contains active links to selected networked resources (both local resources and resources on external networks). Cataloguing has evolved into the process of creating and maintaining resource descriptions (metadata) as the content of resource discovery system. Input to the resource discovery system is based on original cataloguing, bibliographic headers received from publishers, and metadata obtained through co-operative resource description schemes. At a future stage, bibliographic data will also be derived from embedded metadata in networked resources (e.g. URCs).
Resource	In the initial stage, the	At the intermediate	At the developed stage

	Initial stage	Intermediate stage	Developed stage
discovery	library will have an on-line public access catalogue (OPAC) which could be a stand-alone personal computer (in a small library) or a large system with multiple terminals and possibly integrated with other library functions. Bibliographic data contained in the catalogue describes mainly printed resources (e.g. books and journals at the title level), and possibly some other resources such as audio-visual materials and off-line electronic resources.	stage. locally held electronic and networked resources are included in the OPAC, possibly with active links to storage locations. Stand-alone workstations with network browsers are available for access to the global information infrastructure, with pointers to specific knowledge resources and services (gopher, WWW, other libraries).	all storage of electronic resources is based on networked servers and the client-server architecture. There is full network access to all internal and external electronic resources through an integrated resource discovery system. This resource discovery system provides access to carefully selected knowledge resources using sophisticated methods for matching user requests to relevant resources.

	Initial stage	Intermediate stage	Developed stage
User access	Access to the library is mainly limited to on-site access. To a limited extent, requests for service can be sent by telephone, mail or fax, and document delivery is available by mail and fax..	The library catalogue can be accessed over the network, initially using the Telnet protocol, later using the WWW and the Z39.50 protocol. Requests to the library can be sent by e-mail, and document delivery is also available by e-mail as an alternative to postal mail or fax. The library also may offer additional network services, such as an ftp-site (for downloading local resources), and a Gopher or WWW-service which gives access to a limited range of networked resources and support documents.	The library offers both on-site and remote access. On-site access is based on sophisticated tools for identifying and obtaining information. Remote access is based on a 'virtual model' of the physical library, recreating the full functionality of the library on the network in such a way that on-site access is not required for carrying out the full knowledge seeking process. All resources can be delivered to the user over the network, including most printed resources (which are digitised for network delivery).
User support	Support is available from library staff on a face-to-face basis or over the telephone. A printed library guide is available, and perhaps some other support and instructional materials in printed form.	Library systems accessed by users contain an embedded, context-sensitive help-system. Electronic versions of the library guide and systems manuals are available on the library's network service	In addition to human support, the library system offer a fully integrated, computer-assisted support system which can guide the user through the entire process of identifying and accessing knowledge resources. It

	Initial stage	Intermediate stage	Developed stage
		(Gopher or WWW-pages). Specific questions can also be sent to library staff by e-mail.	contains, amongst others, a visual floor-plan of the virtual library, a library guide, system guides and context-sensitive help. For remote users, there is also a real-time interactive conversation system to obtain support from library staff.

Appendix 1: The network infrastructure

20. Appendix 1: The global network infrastructure

20.1 Background information on the Internet

What we refer to as the 'global network infrastructure' or just 'the network' is in fact the result of the merging of many individual networks all over the world, now referred to as the Internet.

The basis of the Internet was formed in the sixties by the network of the US Defense Department, named ARPANET. During the seventies links with other machines in the US and links with the academic sites in the UK and Norway were established. The protocol for data transmission on the Internet (TCP/IP) was finalised in 1982.

The military and defence functions of Arpanet were separated out into a different network, and the National Science Foundation took over the responsibility for the non-military side of the network, later to become NSFnet. During the late 1980s, interconnections were made with EUnet (a European network which connects dozens of countries in Europe) and Aussienet in Australia. National research networks in Europe (JANET in UK, Surfnet in the Netherlands, DFN in Germany and NORDUNET in Scandinavia) made interconnections with the European backbone networks EUnet and EBONE with NSFnet. The networks within different countries are funded and managed locally according to local policies. Recently the NSF has withdrawn its involvement with the Internet. It is now expected that there will be an increasing commercial involvement with the network, enhanced by improved security mechanisms and the emerging of networked payment methods.

In recent years the development in use of the Internet has been very rapid. There now are tens of thousands of connected networks; the number of connected machines rose from several thousands halfway through the eighties to 3 million at the beginning of 1995. The estimated number of Internet users is now between 20 and 30 million.

Networks, and more specifically the Internet form the basis of what has become known as the 'electronic superhighway'. The metaphor has a wider dimension however, pointing to an information society where networks and information services play a predominant role. This concept has found its expression in the 'national information infrastructure' in the United States and the 'European Information Area' in the European Union.

The metaphor of the 'electronic highway' is well chosen: backbone networks such as NSFnet and EUnet can be seen as the highways which connect all kinds of regional and local secondary roads with each other. It is over these roads that the new economic good - information - is transported.

Important organisations: NICs and NOCs

Nobody 'owns' the Internet; there is no single governing body that controls what happens on the Internet. Yet there are many organisations that help manage different parts of the network and to tie everything together. All kinds of national and international networks have their own Network Operations Centre (NOC) and Network Information Centre (NIC). A NOC takes care for the daily functioning of the network; the NIC takes care of user registration and provides assistance to network users.

Every NOC takes care of its own network. A NIC is responsible for the distribution of network addresses and network names. There also is a NIC for the total Internet: InterNIC (Internet Network Information Centre). InterNIC looks after the consistency of Internet as a whole, so that there will be no double names and addresses. InterNIC delegates responsibilities to other organisations. In Europe RIPE (Réseaux IP Européens) is responsible for the technical and administrative co-ordination of the Internet in Europe. RIPE provides basically the same services as InterNIC, but on a European scale. RIPE delegates responsibility to organisations such as EUnet, or national network organisations such as Surfnet in the Netherlands.

The Internet Society

The Internet Society (ISOC) was established in 1992 as an organisation with a kind of final responsibility for the future development of the Internet. The Internet Society, with representatives from the academic and business communities all over the world, is responsible for the promotion of Internet, the developments of the Internet technologies, and for the standardisation of Internet protocols.

Under the umbrella of ISOC, working groups are actively involved in solving Internet-related problems.

- The Internet Architecture Board (IAB) has the final responsibility for the standardisation of the technologies used in Internet.

- The Internet Engineering Task Force (IETF) is involved in short term research and solves existing problems. One important current problem is the explosive growth of the Internet. IETF has several subgroups for various topics, e.g. the URI Group of the IETF develops Uniform Resource Identifiers. They have achieved consensus on the broad details of what is required, though specifics are still being worked out. Another subgroup of the IETF is IAFA (Internet Anonymous FTP Archive) which develops descriptions of resources on anonymous FTP archives.

- The Internet Research Task Force (IRTF) carries out long term research.

The *role of Academic and research institutes and libraries*

Universities and research institutes play an important role in the infrastructure of the Internet. As noted above, Internet consists for an important part of research and academic networks. They also contribute to the development of tools. The University of Minnesota for instance was the birthplace of Gopher, which has its origins in the wish to create a distributed campus information service. CERN (Centre for European Nuclear Research) in Switzerland was the originator of the World Wide Web, which was developed to assist in creating integrated document and information services at CERN.

Libraries have not played an important role in the early development of the Internet. Recently this is starting to change. In the plans for a National Information Infrastructure in the United States, an important role for libraries is foreseen. The Library of Congress was successful in bringing together the most important persons and organisations for a high level meeting on 'delivering electronic information in a knowledge-based democracy'. Also in the US, projects on digital libraries get financial support from the NASA, the Department of Defence and the National Science Foundation. In Europe numerous Internet-related library projects are being carried out, many of which are funded by the European Commission under the Telematics/Library Programme.

20.2 The technical infrastructure of the Internet

Internet protocols

Computers in a network use network protocols, i.e. agreements about the way information on the network will be exchanged and encoded. In the Internet world the so-called TCP/IP protocols are used. These protocols have been implemented for almost all computer operating systems. Therefore, most types of computers can communicate with each other over the network and access each other's resources and services.

The communication between computers on the Internet is handled by the network protocol IP (Internet Protocol). IP serves various tasks, such as identifying computers through their IP-address (a unique identification of a machine on the network) and assuring that data packets are correctly routed from machine to machine. IP is capable of handling a variety of network connections, ranging from Ethernet to X-25 and from analogue telephone networks to digital satellite connections.

The communication between processes, for instance between a database client (where a search query is entered) and a database server (where the requested data is stored), is handled by TCP (Transmission Control Protocol). This illustrates the fact that the Internet is organised according to the client-server principle. This means that a user will use a client programme on his own computer to access services on another computer (the server). A request for service from the client is transmitted over the network to the server, and the result of the request is handed back to the client. Examples of services for which client/server pairs exist are FTP (File Transfer Protocol) for exchanging data files, Electronic Mail (based on SMTP, the Small Mail Transfer Protocol), Usenet News, Gopher (a menu-structured information system), the World Wide Web (WWW, based on the HyperText Transfer Protocol HTTP and the HyperText Mark-up Language HTML) and the Wide Area Information System (WAIS, a mechanism for searching databases on the network). These will be discussed in more detail in the section on 'Internet tools'.

Capacity of the network infrastructure

The success of Internet, reflected in the enormous growth in numbers of users, computer nodes and resources available on the network, has not failed to create problems. These include management and funding, as well as problems in maintaining technical standards, standards of network behaviour etc. But the main problem now facing the Internet world is the lack of access and network capacity. Hosts and modems are often occupied, there is not sufficient access capacity to allow a sufficiently large number of simultaneous users on many sites. The result is often that access has to be denied, especially to FTP-sites. One of the technical problems at this moment is also a lack of bandwidth, i.e. the capacity of the network to carry large amounts of data.

Especially the very popular World Wide Web puts increasing demands on network capacity due to the fact that it involves the transmission of multimedia documents, and therefore of large volumes of data. It is expected that it will take up to three years to resolve these capacity problems and to catch up with demand. The solutions involve not only technical measures (i.e. the installing of high capacity connections), but also organisational approaches. An example of the latter is the development of so-called 'mirror sites', where resources from a site are duplicated at a site in a different geographic area in order to spread the load and to reduce network congestion.

20.3 Internet tools

For its community of users, the Internet serves two distinct functions:

- Providing *communication services* such as electronic mail, news and conversation (through the so-called Internet Relay Chat - IRC). recent developments in this area include real-time video and voice transmission.

- Providing access to a vast array of computer files and other *information resources*.

In order to access information resources, a number of mechanisms have been developed. These include:

- File Transfer (FTP): a mechanism which basically provides access to the directory structure of a remote computer for downloading files stored on that computer. Although FTP is nowadays often accessed through other mechanisms such as Gopher and WWW, the basic FTP mechanism requires knowledge of the exact name and location of a resource to be downloaded.

- Gopher: a menu based system for exploring the Internet. Gopher is presented to the user as a hierarchical structure of menus. Any menu item either leads to a subsequent sub-menu or to an information resource. Sub-menus and information resources accessed through a Gopher service can reside on any computer on the Internet. Thus, choosing a certain menu item on a Gopher in the Netherlands can lead to an information resource (or another Gopher) located in, say, Japan.

- World Wide Web (WWW): a hypertext based information and resource system. The WWW provides access to documents which themselves can contain links to other documents (or services such as Gopher and FTP) anywhere on the network.

WWW documents are multimedia, i.e. they can contain text, images, video and sound.

- Various indexing and search mechanisms for finding resources based on keyword or names searches. These include WAIS (used mainly for searching databases of FTP sites), Veronica (for finding Gopher menus) and an increasing number of WWW searching mechanisms (with names such as ALIWEB, Lycos, WWW Crawler and Yahoo.).

It should be noted that FTP, Gopher and WWW are examples of structures imposed on the vast collection of resources contained within the Internet. They all serve to help users to identify, locate and access resources on the network by offering access to what may be described as distinct *resource spaces*.

For each of these access mechanisms various software tools have been developed, increasingly by commercial software producers. The trend is now towards integration of resource spaces through tools which can access FTP, Gopher and WWW sites. These are generally based on WWW browsers to which FTP and Gopher functionality has been added. Communication functions (e.g. electronic mail and NetNews) are often included as well. These tools can automatically call software for viewing retrieved documents, i.e. viewers for various document types such as word processor formats, SGML, image, audio and video files.

20.4 Standards

A high degree of standardisation is required for discovery, access and retrieval of networked resources. In order to access servers, standards are needed: the so-called access protocols such as HTTP (for the World Wide Web), Gopher, and File Transfer Protocol. In order to discover a resource, a standard description of the resource is required, for instance a Uniform Resource Locator (URL) as discussed in the next chapter.

In order to search for resources in remote databases and on-line catalogues, standards for searching and retrieval have been developed, such as Z39.50 and Search and Retrieve (SR) (ISO 10162/3). These protocols allow use of a standard user interface to access any catalogue or database system on the network in which the protocol has been implemented.

The incorporation of Z39.50 in network access tools such as WWW-browsers is a major improvement on the current TELNET protocol (allowing a terminal client to access a database or OPAC in character mode over the Internet) which has the disadvantage that the user is confronted with the individual system's user interface, language and command or menu structure. The current version of Z39.50 (version 2) supports basic capabilities for bibliographic searching and information retrieval of bibliographic records. It allows the user to build simple and complex search queries using a wide range of qualifiers and search terms. A recently approved new version will support more sophisticated features and incorporate support for both bibliographic and non-bibliographic searching (Turner, 1995). Additional protocols are have been developed for handling transactions between libraries, e.g. for interlibrary lending (covered by ISO 10160/1 ILL)[31].

Networked information resources are available in a wide variety of formats. In addition to pure ASCII and word processor formats, documents can be available in printer formats (Postscript), as structured or hypertext documents (SGML, HTML, HyTime), in so-called portable document formats (ADOBE, Envoy), in image formats (GIF, IFF. JPEG) or as sound or video MPEG, QuickTime). The various types of standards for access to networked resources can therefore be summarised as follows:

Function	Examples	Description
Transmission of information through the Internet	TCP/IP (Internet standards) ISO standards	Protocols for the transmission of data through the network and client/server communication
Communication with services	TELNET (terminal access) SMTP (electronic mail) WAIS FTP Gopher HTTP (WWW)	Protocols for accessing specific types of services or resource spaces on the Internet
Search, retrieve and document delivery	Z39.50 ISO 10161/3 (SR)	Protocols which allow remote access to catalogues and

---

[31] For an overview of OSI standards related to library applications see Hergeth (1995). The problem of linking OSI-based systems with TCP/IP (Internet) applications is discussed by Ciardhuáin (1995). The specific issue of standards in electronic document delivery is discussed by Braid (1995).

Function	Examples	Description
	ISO 10160/1 (ILL)	databases using a uniform user interface, and transactions between libraries
Document identification	Universal Resource Names (URN) Universal Resource Locators (URL) Universal Resource Characteristics (URC)	Means of identifying and describing networked resources and the locations where they are located on the network
Document formats	ASCII Postscript HTML, SGML and HyTime ADOBE GIF, IFF JPEG, MPEG, QuickTime MIME (Multipurpose Internet Mail Extensions: encoding of files attached to electronic mail messages)	Formats for encoding document types (text, structured documents, images, sound, video)

Figure 17: Network standards

Standardisation issues have to be dealt with at an international level. Some are progressing through the international standards organisations, e.g.. the ISO. Others are developed under the control of the Internet Architecture Board (IAB), who has the final responsibility for the standardisation of the technologies used in Internet.

In the library world, work is being carried out in developing, testing and implementing various standards of direct relevance to libraries. Many of these efforts are carried out within the Libraries Programme of the European Commission. Examples are the British/Dutch/French ION project involved with developing interconnections using the ISO search and retrieve and interlibrary loan protocols, the SOCKER project which has as its objective to implement a transportable software communications kernel based on

ISO 10162/3 (SR), and the EDILIBE II project for electronic data interchange between libraries and booksellers.

20.5 Current developments

The World Wide Web is the area of the Internet which is currently creating the most interest. Its use, both as a method of access to networked resources and as a publication channel for hypermedia has increased significantly over the past year. It is in this area that the most interesting technical developments are to be expected. These include:

- HTML (the mark-up language for hypertext documents on the WWW) and HTTP (the transfer protocol used for the WWW) are continually being updated and enhanced. New and future options include the possibility to create and edit documents on a remote server using a local client, and many aspects of presentation (e.g. mathematical equations and formulae, style sheets, document specific toolbars, resizable tables, etc.).

- Other developments are concerned with enhancing the security of the WWW in areas such as access control and data security[32].

- The Common Gateway Interface (CGI), a standard for interfacing external applications with information servers, e.g. HTTP and WWW-servers. By using this mechanism, application systems such as databases can be accessed through the network, e.g. it allows a distant user to query a remote database by entering search terms locally (e.g. via a WWW-browser)[33].

- Hyper-G, developed by the Technical University at Graz, Austria, is a large distributed hypermedia client-server based system which differs from the current WWW-approach in that links between objects are not contained in the objects (e.g. documents) themselves, but are held on a (distributed) link server. This allows for automatic maintenance of the information network. For example, when an object is deleted, the link server can find and delete all links to that object from other objects. In other systems such as Gopher and WWW, it is not easy to find out what documents are pointing to another document, resulting in the all too familiar phenomenon of bad or missing links. In addition, this approach makes it possible

---

[32]   Cf. [http://www.w3.org/hypertext/WWW/Security/Overview.html].
[33]   Cf. [http://www.w3.org/hypertext/WWW/CGI/Overview.html].

to create a graphical representation of the 'surroundings' of a document, to search the link server for specific information, and to control access to objects[34].

- JAVA and HotJava are an approach for creating software programs which can be accessed as networked information resources over the Internet, and which are capable of running on any type of client computer (i.e. locally at the user's desktop). JAVA is the programming language used, and HotJava is a WWW-browser capable of executing JAVA programs[35].

20.6 Network resources

20.6.1 Types and formats of network information resources

Various types of knowledge resources

Network information resource (NIR) is a term used to indicate any information resource which can be accessed on the public networks, notably the Internet. Network information resources include files (documents, software, images), interactive database services (catalogues, directories, etc.), statistical and scientific data sets and any other type of information service. Although in practice the term usually refers to a specific item of information (e.g. a document), it is also used to indicate a collection of documents or other files, e.g. a database or file archive.

Dempsey (1994a) makes a distinction between metadata and resources themselves. Metadata is information about resources, providing some kind of pointer or access route to the resource proper. Some access tools or methods provide access to metadata only (an on-line catalogue, for example), but it is also common that access to metadata and to resources is integrated, and that the path to the resources depends on the organisation of the metadata. To give an example, Archie (a system for finding publicly available files for FTP over the Internet) provides access to a central index of metadata on these files. Archie only returns the address of a file (i.e. the FTP-site, directory and file name) and does not provide access to the resources themselves. Gopher, on the other hand, offers a hierarchical search method which provides direct access to resources from the metadata.

---

[34]   Cf. [http://www.tu-graz.ac.at/].
[35]   Cf. [http://java.sun.com].

There are two levels of metadata:

- Metadata providing information on library resources (i.e. bibliographic records).

- Metadata providing information on catalogues and other bibliographic databases as resources in themselves.

Document types and formats

A resource can consist of text, graphics, sound, images (stills or moving pictures) or a combination of these, so-called multimedia documents. Various formats are used for encoding these different types of information. Some resources are available in word processor format, others in PostScript or portable document formats such as ADOBE/PDF. Graphics, sound and images are available in formats appropriate to the type of resource, as described in the previous section.

An important group of resources is made available through the Word Wide Web. The World Wide Web is based on hypertext and hypermedia documents. Hypertext is basically the same as regular text - it can be stored, read, searched or edited - with an important exception: hypertext documents contain connections or 'links' within the text to other documents. Hypermedia is hypertext with a difference - hypermedia documents contain links not only to other pieces of text, but also to other forms of media: sound, images and movies. Hypermedia therefore combine hypertext and multimedia. The standard language used by the World Wide Web for creating and recognising hypermedia documents is the Hypertext Mark-up Language (HTML), loosely related to, but technically not a subset of, the Standard Generalised Mark-up Language (SGML). HTML and the World Wide Web are important developments for networked information resources. This importance is derived from the fact that HTML offers a combination of functions:

- HTML allows the creation of multimedia documents which are becoming increasingly popular as a publication type;
- HTML functions, through hypertext links, as an access mechanism to resources and services on the network;
- HTML includes special functions for handling transactions over the Internet, e.g. through fill-in forms for entering search requests, ordering information, etc.

As already indicated, the World Wide Web and its related browser software are rapidly becoming the predominant mode of access to the Internet, i.e. not only to the WWW itself but also to other Internet services such as FTP and Gopher, and to databases and catalogues connected to the Internet. In addition, HTML is becoming an important publishing format, i.e. resources available on the network are increasingly being created in HTML format rather than in other, e.g. word processor specific formats.

20.6.2 Resource identification and description

Resource identification

In order to access information, one has to identify the particular information resource desired and determine both how and where it might be used or accessed. Therefore, a method for the unique identification of resources is needed, the so-called URIs (Uniform Resource Identifier). These are developed by the URI Group of the IETF. URIs make it possible to refer to resources and to share information about resources. URIs facilitate the development of network publishing, support a variety of links (hypertextual, between a description and the objects it describes) and provide a core for electronic citations as a form of 'bibliographic descriptions' of networked information resources.

An identifier has ideally three components: a Uniform Resource Name (URN), Uniform Resource Locators (URL) and Uniform Resource Citation or Characteristics (URC):

URN: A URN identifies a resource or unit of information. The purpose or function of a URN is to provide a unique, unchanging identifier used for recognition, for access to descriptions of the resource or for access to the resource itself (the bibliographic analogue is an ISBN). The resource identified by a URN can reside in one or more locations at any given time, may move, or may not be available at all. Of course, not all resources will move during their lifetime, and not all resources, although identifiable and identified by a URN will be instantiated at any given time.

URL A URL identifies the location of a resource on the network. A URL also includes a parameter that describes the type of service used to retrieve a particular information object (e.g. FTP, Gopher or WWW). As such, a URL identifies a location where a resource may reside, a 'container', as distinct from the resource itself identified by the URN.

URC A URC is a set of meta-level information about a resource. Some examples of such meta-information are: owner, encoding, access restrictions (perhaps for particular instances), cost. (Sollins & Masinter, 1994)

A complete URI therefore consists of a unique resource 'name' (URN), the locations where the resource can be obtained, including access information (one or more URLs) and additional descriptive information (URC).

There is an increasing use of URLs in citations to electronic resources. URLs can be interpreted by World Wide Web clients which will act on a user-supplied URL, or on the URL contained within an HTML document. The use of URLs is still experimental, but there is a strong backing from the tool-developers. The concept of a URN is less stable and URNs are not yet commonly used. Mechanisms which will allow URNs to be translated into URLs are being worked out.

Resource description

An unique identifier is necessary for finding networked information resources. Ways of resource description will assist users in finding resources. However, current Internet resource discovery systems poorly describe resources. One can easily waste a lot of time obtaining a resource which turns out to be irrelevant or unusable because the appropriate software for viewing it is not available. There is also not a clear way to assess the quality of the resource. With paper resources one can judge the quality and usability of a document on the basis of information about the publisher, edition (paperback or hard bound), etc. Networked resources usually have to be obtained from their source before one can see if it is what one needs.

There is a need for improving resource description, including more variety of attributes that characterise resources, for example the size of an object, its type and quality. It is a problem to establish a format for resource descriptions because features that need to be described are complex or immature, because it not clear in what way users want to search for resources, and because new types of resources are appearing and the whole concept of an electronic document is changing. Therefore, standardisation of resource description is premature. There have been several attempts for standard description. From the library-side there are some attempts to integrate 'traditional' cataloguing standards with networked resources description[36]. The IAFA Group of IETF has identified a number of objects for description of resources, such as user, organisation, site information, document, image, etc. They have also defined templates consisting of multiple attribute-value pairs. These templates are used to create fuller descriptions in the network environment. Another promising approach is from the Text Encoding Initiative: The Text Encoding Initiative has produced a framework for the documentation and interchange of electronic texts based on SGML. A TEI header (which includes data such as title, edition, publication, revisions, etc.) has been developed in reference to library descriptive standards (for example International Standard Book Description, the Anglo-American Cataloguing Rules, 2nd edition and MARC records).

There are two different approaches for the creation of resource descriptions:

- Automatic searching for and extraction of metadata based on the existing content or characteristic of resources.

- Individually cataloguing of Internet resources based on human inspection.

Of course, a combination of these two approaches is possible.

Dempsey (1944a) characterises the current situation with regard to resource description as follows:

- Creation: descriptive metadata can be extracted from existing titles, locations, or other resource characteristics (e.g. Archie, Veronica, various robots and Web wanderers). Metadata (e.g. WAIS sources, TEI headers, IAFA templates) can be manually created by information providers, or it can be created by other parties (e.g. libraries).

- Content: metadata is typically very sparse, unstructured and is often hidden (e.g. in README or INDEX files which describe a set of resources). There are moves to enhance the content in various ways: providing facilities for extra descriptive information (e.g. in Gopher +); growing attention to agreed, fuller formats, more sophisticated post-processing of available data, or more active searching out and consolidation of metadata.

---

[36]   See for example Library of Congress Network Development and Standards Office (1995).

- Propagation: resource descriptions can be collected automatically by software (e.g. ALIWEB, Archie, Veronica), collected manually, or be manually 'forwarded' to some agency. They can also sit alongside the resource, to be processed in different ways (e.g. Z39.50 'explain' service; Gopher menus; HTML Home pages). It has been proposed to use the Domain Name System (distributed naming system) for propagation of identifying metadata or URIs.

- Organisation: resource descriptions can be presented as a directed graph, as a searchable index, or distributed in some form of directory service. The latter is likely to become more important.

- Access: typically search (through queries to a database) or browse (using network navigation tools).

20.6.3 Further development of a network information system

The development of global, sustainable resource discovery systems is a necessary component of a global network information system. The actual design and construction

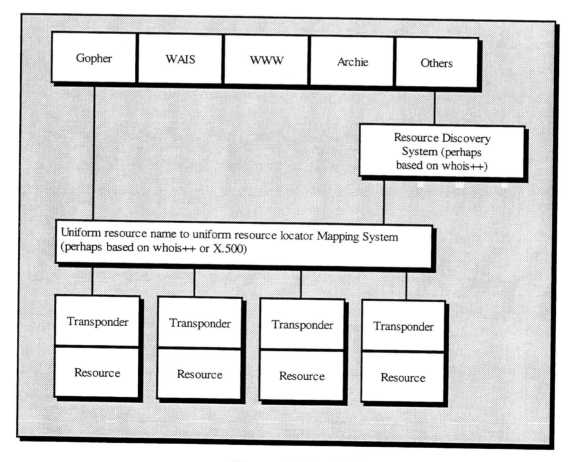

Figure 18: A global network information system

are still matters for research and development. Weider and Deutsch (1944a) present a vision of integration:

This schema has been proposed within the integration on Internet Information Resources Working Group of the IETF as 'a vision' of how services might be integrated and developed.

Four levels are proposed:

- Resources themselves. Each resource should have a Uniform Resource Name.

- A directory service which resolves names into locators (a resource may have several locations, described by URLs).

- A resource discovery system. This would be a searchable database of resource descriptions, allowing the user to discover the URNs of relevant resources. (Of course, if a name or location is already known, the discovery and name to locator services would not be required). WHOIS++ is a lightweight directory service which is currently being developed; it is not yet widely deployed but is seen by some as a substitute for slowly developing X.500 services for address directories.

- Access and delivery tools, e.g. Gopher and WWW software.

Dempsey identifies an important trend of integration of Internet resource discovery systems. There are three current strands of activity here:

- The construction of 'gateways' between current Internet access and discovery tools and between these tools and other resources.

- The development of agreed approaches to naming, addressing and describing resources to facilitate the propagation of information about resources.

- The development of agreed formats for document interchange.

APPENDIX 2: KNOWLEDGE MEDIATION CONCEPTS

21. Appendix 2: Knowledge mediation concepts

In this appendix we identify a number of concepts[37] which have been used in our analysis of knowledge mediation. This list can also be used as a checklist of items for describing the knowledge mediation function of any individual library.

1 *Knowledge mediation*

Knowledge mediation is the process whereby libraries provide users insight into the existing body of knowledge and assist users in acquiring resources referring to or containing such knowledge.

2 *Information resources*

Information resources are information items available to users in the knowledge mediation process. Information resources consist of two distinct categories:

2.1 Knowledge resources

Knowledge resources (normally described as 'publications' or 'documents') are information resources in which knowledge is represented and through which knowledge is transferred to users. Knowledge resources can belong to any of the following basic types:

> 2.1.1 Printed books and journals available for on-site consultation, loan or photocopying, either held by the user's own library or available from other libraries or document delivery services

> 2.1.2 Audio-visual materials, microforms etc., accessible through specific playing or viewing devices

> 2.1.3 Off-line electronic media (e.g. CD-ROM, CD-I), accessible on a stand-alone machine or through a local network

> 2.1.4 Electronic documents on local servers, accessible through the local network

---

[37] These concepts are derived from the desk research carried out in Phase 1 of the Knowledge Models project.

2.1.5 Electronic documents in on-line databases, accessible through on-line hosts

2.1.6 Electronic resources on the global network (in general the Internet)

2.2   Reference resources

Reference resources are (sets of) information resources which describe knowledge resources. Reference resources contain at least a formal description of the knowledge resource (e.g. bibliographic descriptions identifying title, author, etc.) and possibly subject descriptors and/or resource locators (pointers to one or more locations where the resource can be obtained).

NB: in some cases reference resources are combined with knowledge resources (e.g. in full-text databases) or with a summary of the knowledge resource (e.g. in abstract journals or databases).

In this analysis reference resources are regarded as a component of *resource discovery mechanisms* (cf. concept 5).

3   *Knowledge resource locations*

The resources identified by a resource discovery mechanism can be categorised according to their location (i.e. the place where they can be obtained):

3.1   Resources available in the user's own library (e.g. identified through a catalogue or journal list)

3.2   Resources directly available from on-line or networked source (e.g. identified through a network browse or search mechanism)

3.3   Resources available from other libraries (e.g. identified through a union catalogue or remote access library catalogue)

3.4   Resources without reference to location, possibly available in the user's own library (e.g. identified though a printed bibliography or bibliographic database)

4 *Resource discovery*

Resource discovery is the process by which users find knowledge resources relevant to their knowledge needs.

4.1 Resource identification

Resource identification is the process by which users obtain knowledge of the existence and identity of specific knowledge resources.

4.2 Resource locating

Resource locating is the process by which users obtain knowledge of the location of knowledge resources, i.e. the place where they are held and can be obtained.

5 *Resource discovery mechanisms*

Resource discovery mechanisms are supporting mechanisms for carrying out resource discovery. The purpose of a resource discovery mechanism is to help the user identify and locate knowledge resources pertaining to a specific information seeking task. They consist of the following components:

- reference resources
  - document descriptions
  - subject descriptors
  - resource locators

- indexed search and/or sorted, hierarchical or hyperlink browse mechanism

- interface for using the mechanism, presenting reference resources and in some cases also accessing the identified knowledge resources

An important issue in the context of resource discovery mechanisms is the extent to which they are integrated into a single (automated) system in order to minimise a priori choices (cf. section 0).

The most commonly used types of resource discovery mechanisms can be categorised as follows[38]:

5.1 Internal resource discovery mechanisms (maintained by the library)

    5.1.1 Structured physical arrangement of resources (e.g. a subject-oriented arrangement of physical materials on the stacks)

    5.1.2 Catalogues providing entry points (e.g. author, title, subject etc.) to reference resources (document descriptions) referring to their physical location

    5.1.3 Subject or course oriented listings, lists of recent acquisitions

    5.1.4 Electronic lists or catalogues of networked information resources, referring to their network location

    5.1.5 Bibliographies and other reference works in the library
        5.1.5.1   Printed form
        5.1.5.2   CD-ROM based

    5.1.6 Publisher catalogues and Books-in-Print publications

    5.1.7 Knowledge resources (e.g. books and journal articles) containing bibliographic references or (in the case of electronic documents) referring to networked resources

5.2 External resource discovery mechanisms (maintained by others)

    5.2.1 Other library catalogues (incl. union catalogues)
    5.2.2 On-line databases maintained by host organisations
    5.2.3 Catalogues and books-in-print lists maintained by publishers
    5.2.4 Network browsing mechanisms which allow the user to browse through resource spaces structured by methods such as directories, hierarchies and hypertext links (FTP, Gopher, WWW, etc.)

---

[38]   It should be noted that the following list only describes categories or types. In practice, the library user can choose from various specific alternatives for each type, e.g. from a number of different catalogues, bibliographies, CD-ROMs, on-line databases, network browsing mechanisms, etc.

5.2.5 Network search mechanisms: searchable indexes of electronic resources on the network

6 *Resource selection*

Resource selection is the process of selecting resources from a set of available alternatives.

6.1 Selecting resources from those identified
6.2 Selecting appropriate location if alternatives exist
6.3 Selecting appropriate form if alternatives exist

7 *Resource delivery*

Resource delivery is the process of making knowledge resources physically available to the user.

7.1 Resource provision

Resource provision is the process of making a knowledge resource available in the user's library

Resource provision methods include:

7.1.1 provide from library collection
7.1.2 provide from other library (via ILL)
7.1.3 provide from document provider
7.1.4 download from network

7.2 Resource transfer

Resource transfer is the process of transferring (a copy of) a knowledge resource from its location to the user.

Resource transfer methods include:

7.2.1 on-site access and consultation
7.2.2 photocopy

7.2.3 fax

7.2.4 (e)mail

7.2.5 download from network to user (e.g. via FTP, Gopher or WWW)

8 *Knowledge mediation decisions*

The knowledge mediation function presents the user with many decisions in carrying out the process of finding and obtaining information resources. The main types of choices where such decisions have to be made are:

8.1 Choice of resource discovery mechanism(s)

8.2 Choice of alternative resource form(s) and media (e.g. print or electronic, CD-ROM or on-line)

8.3 Choice of resource location

8.4 Choice of delivery option

9 *Quality issues*

9.1 Quality of resources

9.1.1 Quality of content

9.1.1.1   Subject matter / relevance

9.1.1.2   Reliability

9.1.2 Timeliness

9.1.3 Availability

9.1.4 Cost

9.1.5 Language

9.2 Quality of discovery mechanisms

9.2.1 Ease of use

9.2.2 Coverage / recall

9.2.3 Selectivity / precision

9.2.4 Language (incl. multilingual character sets)

9.3 Quality of network access

9.3.1 Availability

9.3.2 Speed

9.3.3 Cost

9.4   Quality of library service

9.4.1 Coverage of resources

9.4.2 Available resource discovery mechanisms

9.4.3 Ease of use

9.4.4 Quality of user-support

9.4.5 Speed of service

9.4.6 Cost to user

9.5   Quality assessment

9.6   Quality control

10 *Libraries*

10.1 Library types

10.1.1   Public libraries

10.1.2   Academic libraries

10.1.3   Special libraries

10.1.4   National libraries

10.2 Other organisations

10.2.1   Resource publishers

10.2.2   Booksellers

10.2.3   Subscription agents

10.2.4   Host organisations

10.2.5   Information brokers

10.2.6   Document delivery agents

10.2.7   Library systems suppliers

10.2.8   Co-operative library networks

10.2.9   Network infrastructure providers

10.3 Library processes

      10.3.1   Acquisition

      10.3.2   Reference, cataloguing and indexing

      10.3.3   Lending and document delivery

      10.3.4   User support

            10.3.4.1   Personal assistance

            10.3.4.2   Distance support

            10.3.4.3   Manuals, resource guides etc.

            10.3.4.4   On-line help

            10.3.4.5   Instruction and computerised training

            10.3.4.6   Signposting

            10.3.4.7   Resource descriptions

11 *Library users*

11.1 User type

11.2 User location

      11.2.1   In user's own library

      11.2.2   In other library

      11.2.3   Distance access user (from home or office)

12 *Networks*

12.1 Network type

      12.1.1   Internal (local) library network

      12.1.2   Institutional network

      12.1.3   Co-operative library network

      12.1.4   Global network infrastructure

12.2 Network organisations

      12.2.1   Library network organisations

12.2.2　　Internet organisations

     12.2.2.1　Network Operations centres

     12.2.2.2　Network Information centres

12.2.3　　Network access providers

12.3　Networked resources (sub-set of 2.1.6)

12.4　Network tools

    12.4.1　　Communication tools

       12.4.1.1　E-mail clients

       12.4.1.2　IRC clients

    12.4.2　　Information tools

       12.4.2.1　Browsers

         12.4.2.1.1　FTP clients

         12.4.2.1.2　Gopher clients

         12.4.2.1.3　WWW clients

       12.4.2.2　Viewers

         12.4.2.2.1　Viewers for media formats (images, video, sound)

         12.4.2.2.2　Viewers for document formats (e.g. postscript, SGML, PDF)

       12.4.2.3　Search tools

         12.4.2.3.1　Telnet interfaces to library catalogues and on-line databases

         12.4.2.3.2　Z39.50 interfaces to library catalogues and on-line databases

         12.4.2.3.3　Network index and search tools

BIBLIOGRAPHY

22. Bibliography

Ackerman, M. S.; Fielding, R. T. (1995) - Collection maintenance in the digital library. - Paper presented at Digital Libraries 95. - [http://csdl.tamu.edu/DL95/papers/ackerman/ackerman.html].

Adie, Chris (1993). - A survey of distributed multimedia research, standards and products. - RARE Technical Report, 5.

Agre, Phil (1994) - Networking on the network. - San Diego: University of California, Department of Communication.

Allen, Bryce (1994). - Cognitive abilities and information system usability. - In: Information processing & management, 30(2), 177-191.

American Library Association Telecommunications and Information Infrastructure Policy Forum Proceedings (1993). - Principles for the development of the National Information Infrastructure. - Washington, DC: September 8 - 10, 1993.

Anderson, Christopher (1995). - The accidental superhighway. [http://www.economist.com/surveys/internet/index.html].

Andreesen, Marc (1994). - A beginner's guide to URLs. [FTP://ftp.ncsa.uiuc.edu/Web/mosaic-papers/url-primer.ps.Z].

Arms, W.Y. (1995). - Key concepts in the architecture of the digital library. - In: Dlib magazine, July 1995. - [http://www.cnri.reston.va.us/home/dlib/July95/07arms.html].

Arnold, K. - The body in the virtual library: rethinking scholarly communication.- In: Teresa harrison, Timothy Stephen, Computer networking andscholarship in the 21th century university. - New York: State University of New York Press. - [http://www.press.umich.edu/jep/works/arnold.body.html].

Baker, S. ; Jackson, M. E. (1993). - Maximizing access, minimizing cost: a first step toward the information access future. - Prepared for the ARL Committee on Access to Information Resources.

Barry, C. L. (1994). - User-defined relevance criteria: an exploratory study. - In: Journal of the American Society for Information Science, 45(3), 149-159.

Batt, Chris (1995). - The library of the future: public libraries and the Internet. - Paper for the 61st IFLA General Conference, August 2-25.
[http://www.nlc-bnc.ca/ifla/IV/ifla61/61-batc.htm]

Berners-Lee, Tim et al. (1992). - World-Wide Web: The Information Universe. - In: Electronic networking: research, applications and policy, vol. 2, no. 1, pp. 52-58.

Berners-Lee, Tim, Larry Masinter and Mark McCahill. (1994). - Uniform Resource Locators. Internet Draft version (22 July 1994).
[FTP://nic.nordu.net/internet-drafts/draft-ietf-uri-url-06.txt].

Berry, J.W. (1995). - Digital libraries: new initiatives with world wide implications. - Paper presented at the 61st IFLA General Conference. -
[http://www.nlc-bnc.ca/ifla/IV/ifla61/61-berjo.htm].

Billington, James H. (1994). - The electronic library. - In: Media studies journal, Winter 1994, 109 - 112.

Bos, Bert (1993). - An information infrastructure for a Faculty of Arts: an analysis and a proposal. - The Hague, NBBI.

Boutell, Thomas (1994). - World Wide Web Frequently Asked Questions.

Braid, Andrew (1995). - Standardisation in electronic document delivery. - In: Geh, Hans-Peter and Marc Walckiers (eds) (1995). - Proceedings of the European Conference 'Library networking in Europe', Brussels, 12-14 October 1994, 157-166.

British Library Working Party on Electronic Publishing (1994). - The impact of electronic publishing on library services and resources in the UK.

Broadbent, Marianne and Lofgren, Hans (1993). - Information delivery: identifying priorities, performance, and value. - In: Information processing & management, 29(6), 683-701.

Browning, J. (1994). - Libraries without walls for books without pages. - In: Wired 1.1: Library of the Future.

Cameron, R.D. (1994). - To link or to copy: Four principles for materials acquisition in Internet electronic libraries. - (CMPT TR 94-08). - [http://fas.sfu.ca/0/projects/ElectronicLibrary/project/papers/e-lib-links.html].

Caplan, Priscilla (1993). - Cataloging internet resources. - In: Public-access computer systems review, 4(2), 61-66.

Chaudry, A.S. (1995). - Exploiting network information resources for collection development in libraries. - Paper presented at the 61st IFLA General Conference. - [http://www.nlc-bnc.ca/ifla/IV/ifla61/61-chaa.htm].

Ciardhuáin, Séamus Ó (1995). - A multifunctional gateway for information retrieval protocols. - In: Geh, Hans-Peter and Marc Walckiers (eds) (1995). - Proceedings of the European Conference 'Library networking in Europe', Brussels, 12-14 October 1994, p. 147-155.

Clement, Gail P. (1994). - Library without walls. In: Internet world, 5(6):60-64.

Cleveland, G. (1995). - Overview of document management technology. - (UDT Occasional paper, 2). [http://www.nlc-bnc.ca/ifla/pubs/core/udt/occasional/udtop.htm].

Common Gateway Interface. - [http://www.w3.org/hypertext/WWW/CGI/Overvbiew.html].

Cousins, S. B. e.a. (1995) - InterPay: managing multiple payment mechanisms in digital libraries. - Paper presented at Digital Libraries 95. - [http://csdl.tamu.edu/DL95/papers/cousins/cousins.html].

Crocca, W. T. ; Anderson, W. L. - delivering technology for digital libraries: experience as vendors. Paper presented at Digital Libraries 95. - [http://csdl.tamu.edi/papers/crocca/crocca.html].

Cummings, Anthony M.; Marcia L. Witte, William G. Bowen, Laura O. Lazarus, and Richard EKMAN. (1992). - University libraries and scholarly communication. -

Published by The Association of Research Libraries for The Andrew W. Mellon Foundation. November 1992.

Daniel, Ron jr. (1994a). - A global distributed directory service for the World Wide Web.
[http://www.acl.lanl.gov/URI/DistURC/parser.C.]

Daniel, Ron jr. (1994b). - Proposed URC external representation.
[http://www.acl.lanl.gov/URI/ExtReo/urc0.HTML]

Danilowicz, Czaslaw (1994). - Modelling of user preferences and needs in boolean retrieval systems. - In: Information processing & management, 30(3), 363-378.

Davenport, Elisabeth (1994). - Perception of economics in a digital publishing environment. A report on a field study. - In: Interlending & document supply, 22(4), 8-16.

Davies, James R. & Lagoze, Carl (1994). - A protocol and server for a distributed digital technical report library.

Davies, M. (1994). - CWIS-like developments at the Imperial Cancer Research Institute. - In: Serials, 7(2).

De Kock, Martie (1993). - Remote users of an online public access catalogue (OPAC): problems and support. - In: Electronic Library, 11(4/5), 241-243. users needs.

December, John (1994a) - Internet-Tools.
[FTP://ftp.rpi.edu/pub/communications/internet-tools.html]

December, John (1994b). - Internet-CMC.
[FTP://ftp.rpi.edu/pub/communications/internet-cmc.html]

Dempsey, Lorcan (1994a). - Network resource discovery: a European library perspective. In: Neil Smith (ed). - Libraries, networks and Europe: a European networking study. - London, England: British Library R & D Department.

Dempsey, Lorcan (1994b) - Distributed library and information systems: the significance of Z39.50. In: managing information, 1(6):41-43.

Dempsey, Lorcan (1995). - RADAR Reflections: Internet Resource, Access, Discovery and Retrieval Systems and Libraries. - In: Geh, Hans-Peter and Marc Walckiers (eds) (1995). - Proceedings of the European Conference 'Library networking in Europe', Brussels, 12-14 October 1994, 67-81.

Dempsey, Lorcan (ed.) (1992). - Library bibliographic networks in Europe: a LIBER directory. - The Hague: NBLC.

Dempsey, Lorcan; Ann Mumford and Bill Tuck (1993). - Standards of relevance to networked library services. - In: Libraries and IT: working papers of the Information Technology Subcommittee of the HEFC's Libraries Review. - Bath: UKOLN.

Deutsch, Peter (1992). - Resource discovery in an Internet environment: the Archie approach. - In: Electronic networking: research, applications and policy, 2(1): 45-51.

Dillon, Martin, Erik Jul, Mark Burge, Carol Hickey (1993). - Assessing information on the Internet: toward providing library services for computer-mediated communication. - Dublin, Oh.: OCLC Office of Research, 1993.

Duckett, Bob (1994). - Do users matter?. In: Cataloguing and Indexing Group of the Library Association in London (ed.), Catalogue & index (pp. 1-8). London: Cataloguing and Indexing Group.

Dugall, Berndt (1995). - EDILIBE II: steps towards OSI-based electronic business relations between libraries and booksellers. - In: Geh, Hans-Peter and Marc Walckiers (eds) (1995). - Proceedings of the European Conference 'Library networking in Europe', Brussels, 12-14 October 1994, p. 185-191.

Eekhout, A., Koster, L., Putman, E. (1993). - Documentaire dienstverlening en klanttevredenheid. - In: Open, 25(11), 398-399.

European Commission, Directorate General XIII (1994). - The Internet and the European information industry. - Luxembourg, IMO. - IMO Working Paper 94/3.

European Commission, Directorate General XIII (1995). - Telematics Applications Programme 1994-1998. Telematics for Libraries. DGXIII.

European Commission, Directorate General XIII, Information Market Observatory (1995). - The quality of electronic information products and services. - Luxembourg: IMO. - (IMO Working Paper 95/4).

Flynn, K.M. (1995). - The knowledge manager as a digital librarian: an overview of the Knowledge Management Pilot Program at the MITRE Corporation. - Paper presented at Digital Libraries 95. -
[http://csdl.tamu.edu/DL95/papers/flynn/flynn.html].

Foster, Jullie (ed.) (994). - A status report on networked information retrieval: tools and groups.
[FTP://nic.nordu.net/Internet-drafts/draft-ietf-nir-status-report-03.txt]

Frappaolo, Carl (1992). - What do users want from an online system?. - In: Online Meeting, Proceedings, 13, 115-116.

Gaynor, Edward (1994). - The documentation of electronic texts using Text Encoding Initiative headers: an introduction. - In: Library resources and technical services, 38(4):389-401.

Geh, Hans-Peter and Marc Walckiers (eds) (1995). - Proceedings of the European Conference 'Library networking in Europe', Brussels, 12-14 October 1994.

Ghani, D. (1995). - Charging and paying for information on open networks. - In: ASLIB proceedings, 47(6):145-158.

Gladney, Henry M. e.a. (1994). - Digital library: gross structure and requirements: report from a March 1994 Workshop. - In: Proceedings of the First Annual Conference on the Theory and Practice of Digital Libraries, June 19-21, College Station, Texas, USA.
[http://atg1.wustl.edu/DL94/]

Gotze, Dietrich Springer Verlag (1994). - Electronic journals: market and technology. - In: STM Newsletter(94), 7-17.

Gourlay, U, ; Vattulainen, P. (1995) - The changing roles of document delivery and interlending in libraries. - Paper presented at the 61st IFLA General Conference. -
[http://www.nlc-bnc.ca/ifla/IV/ifla61/61-gouu.htm].

Graham, P. (1994). - The mid-decade catalog and its environment. - Pre-print draft. - [http://aultnis.rutgers.edu/texts/cffc.html].

Graham, P. (1995). - Bibliography on electronic library issues. - [http://aultnis.rutgers.edu/texts/ElectBib.html].

Graham, P. (1995). - Requirements for the digital research library. - In: College and research Libraries, July 1995, p. 331-339. - [http://aultnis.rutgers.edu/texts/DRC.html].

Graham, P. (1995). - Why there will be no special collections on the Internet. - [http://aultnis.rutgers.edu/texts/RBS1995talk.html].

Griffiths, José-Marie and Kimberly K. Kertis (1994). - Access to large digital libraries of scientific information across networks. - In: Proceedings of the First Annual Conference on the Theory and Practice of Digital Libraries, June 19-21, College Station, Texas, USA.
[http://atg1.wustl.edu/DL94/]

Guedon, J.-C. (1994). - Why are electronic publications difficult to classify? The orthogonality of print and digital media. - [http://www.nlc-bnc.ca/documents/libraries/cataloging/guej1.txt].

Harnad, S. (1995). - Electronic scholarly publication: quo vadis. - In: Managing Information, 2, March, 3, 31-33.

Harris, Donald E. (1994). - Reassessing user needs. - In: Journal of the American Society for Information Science, 45(5), 331-334.

Hart, P.J. and Rice, R.E. (1991). - Using information from external databases: contextual relationships of use, access method, task, database type, organizational differences, and outcomes. - In: Information processing & Management, 27(5), 461-479.

Hawks, C.P. (1995). - OhioLINK: implementing integrated library services across institutional boundaries. - In: The public-access computer systems review, (6)2.

Hepworth, Marc (1994). - Singapore's Library 2000 Report.

Hergeth, Bernd (1995). - OSI in the field of library applications. - In: Geh, Hans-Peter and Marc Walckiers (eds) (1995). - Proceedings of the European Conference 'Library networking in Europe', Brussels, 12-14 October 1994, p. 123-146.

Hernon, Peter and Charles R. McClure. (1993). - Electronic U.S. Government information: policy issues and directions. - In: Annual Review of Information Science and Technology (ARIST). Medford, NJ: Learned Information, Inc. Volume 28, 1993: 45 - 110.

Herpay, Eva (1991). - Meeting the user's need: the most important task of the information specialist. - In: Quarterly Bulletin of the International Association of Agricultural Information Specialists, 36(1-2), 44-45.

Hockey, Susan (1993). - Developing access to electronic texts in the humanities. - In: Computers in libraries, 38(2):41-43.

Hoogcarspel, Annelies (1994). Guidelines for cataloging monographic electronic texts at the Center for Electronic Texts in the Humanities. Technical Report no. 1. New Brunswick, NJ: Center for Electronic Texts in the Humanities.

Hugenholtz, Bernt (1995). - Copyright problems of electronic document delivery. - In: Geh, Hans-Peter and Marc Walckiers (eds) (1995). - Proceedings of the European Conference 'Library networking in Europe', Brussels, 12-14 October 1994, p. 349-358.

Hughes, Kevin (1994). - Entering the World-Wide Web: A guide to cyberspace. - Enterprise Integration Technologies, May 1994.

Hyper-G. - [http://hyperg.tu-graz.ac.at/].

Information Infrastructure Task Force. (1993). - The National Information Infrastructure: agenda for action. Washington, DC: Department of Commerce.

International Federation of Library Associations. - Digital libraries resources and projects.
[http://www.nlc-bnc.ca/ifla/II/diglib.htm].

International Federation of Library Associations. - Interlibrary loan, document delivery and resource sharing information.
[http://www.nlc-bnc.ca/ifla/II/ill.htm].

International Federation of Library Associations. - Cataloguing and indexing of electronic resources.
[http://www.nlc-bnc.ca/ifla/II/catalog.htm].

James-Catalano, Cynthia N. (1995). - The virtual library. - In: Internet World., 6(6), 26-28.

Joint Information Systems Committee (JICS) (1995). - Electronic libraries programme. - [http://ukoln.bath.ac.uk/elib/wk_papers/figit-11-95.html].

Jorgensen, Poul Henrik (1995). - Transportable OSI Search and Retrieve implementation in the SOCKER Project. - In: Geh, Hans-Peter and Marc Walckiers (eds) (1995). - Proceedings of the European Conference 'Library networking in Europe', Brussels, 12-14 October 1994, p. 167-178.

Kahin, B. (1994). - Institutional and policy issues in the development of the digital library. - In: International conference on Scholarship and technology in the humanities, April. -
[http://www.press.umich.edu/jep/works/kahin.dl.html].

Kahle, Brewster (1992). - Electronic publishing and public libraries. - The Reading Room, Digital Media - A Seybold Report. February 1992.

Kahle, Brewster et al. (1992) - Wide Area Information Servers: An executive information system for unstructured files.- In: Electronic Networking: Research, Applications and Policy , 2(1):59-68.

Kahn, R. ; Wilensky, R. (1994). - Locating electronic library services and objects: a frame of reference for the CS-TR Project (draft for discussion purposes). -
[http://www.nlc-bnc.ca/documents/libraries/cataloging/metadata/handles2.txt].

Kambitsch, Tim (1994). - Mainstreaming our library catalogs. -
[http://www.butler.edu/www/library/papers/lotf.html].

Kling, Rob (1994). - Institutional and organizational dimensions of the effective use of digital libraries: brief project description. - in: ASIS-L digests.

Klobas, Jane E. (1993). - So why do people use online? An investigation of discretionary use of electronic information resources. - In: Online Information, 219-226.

Koster, Martijn (1994). ALIWEB - Archie-like indexing in the Web. [http://info.webcrawler.com/mak/projects/aliweb/paper-www94/].

Kritz, Harry M. (1994) - Teaching and publishing in the World Wide Web. - Virginia Polytechnic Institute and State University. - cf: [http://learning.lib/vt/edu/authors/hmkriz.html].

Kurzweil, Raymond. (1992a). - The future of libraries Part 1: the technology of the book. - In: Library journal: January 1992, 80 - 82.

Kurzweil, Raymond. (1992b). - The Future of libraries Part 2: the end of books. - In: Library journal: February 15, 1992, 140 - 142.

Kurzweil, Raymond. (1992c). - The Future of libraries Part 3: the virtual library. - In: Library journal: March 15, 1992, 63 - 64.

Kurzweil, Raymond. (1993). - The virtual book revisited. - In: Library journal: February 15, 1993, 145 - 146.

Lago, Karen Nadder. (1993). - The Internet and the public library: practical and political realities. In: Internet librarian: October, 1993.

Lamb, R. (1995). - Using online information resources: reaching for the *.*'s. - Paper presented at Digital Libraries 95. - [http://csdl.tamu.edu/DL95/papers/lamb/lamb.html].

Langer, P. & Wilson, A.J.C. (1994). - Online user needs in chemical information. - In: Journal of chemical information and computer sciences, 34(4), 707-713.

Law, Derek (1995). - Empowering the end-user: networked services and national information policy. - In: Geh, Hans-Peter and Marc Walckiers (eds) (1995). -

Proceedings of the European Conference 'Library networking in Europe', Brussels, 12-14 October 1994, p. 219-225.

Lehmann, Klaus-Dieter (1995). - Networking and the challenges to be faced. - In: Geh, Hans-Peter and Marc Walckiers (eds) (1995). - Proceedings of the European Conference 'Library networking in Europe', Brussels, 12-14 October 1994, p. 365-375.

Levy, David M. & Marshall, Catherine C. (1995). - Going digital: A look at assumptions underlying digital libraries. - In: Communications of the ACM, 38(4), 77-84.

Libraries and the NII - Draft for public comment. (1994).

Library Information enquiry and Referral Network (1994). - Project LIRN. - Press release.

Library of Congress Network Development and MARC Standards Office (1994). - USMARC format for bibliographic data: including Guidelines for content designation. 1994 edition. Washington: Library of Congress.

Library of Congress Network Development and Standards Office (1995). - Providing access to online information resources: discussion paper. - MARBI Discussion Paper no. 54.
[http://www.nlc-bnc.ca/documents/libraries/cataloging/marbi54.txt].

Line, M.B. (1995). - Acces vs. ownership: how real an alternative is it? - Paper presented at the 61st IFLA General Conference. -
[http://www.nlc-bnc.ca/ifla/IV/ifla61/61-linm.htm].

Lopata, Cynthia L. and Charles R. McClure (1994). - Assessing the impacts of the Internet/NREN networking on the academic institution. - News release.

Luijendijk, Wim C. (1994). - IT (Information Technology) ain't necessarily so ... - In: International forum on information and documentation, 19(1), 19-31.

Lupovici, Ch. (1995). - Normes et édition électronique. - Paper presented at the 61st IFLA General Conference. -
[http://www.nlc-bnc.ca/ifla/ifla61/61-lupc.htm].

Luyt-Prinsen, Jola G.B. van (1995). - Abonnees over Exerpta Informatica: Een gebruikersonderzoek bij het commerciële documentatiecentrum van de KUB-bibliotheek. - In: Open, 27(4), 125-127.

Lyman, Peter. (1991). - The library of the (not-so-distant) future. - In: Change: January/February 1991, 34 - 41.

Lynch, Clifford A. (1993a). - Interoperability: the standards challenge for the 1990s. In: Wilson library bulletin, March 1993.

Lynch, Clifford A. (1993b). - The roles of libraries in access to networked information: cautionary tales from the era of broadcasting. - Paper based on a presentation given at the Data Processing Conference in Champaign-Urbana, April 5, 1993.

Lynch, Clifford A. (1993c). - A framework for identifying, locating and describing networked information resources.
[FTP://ftp.cni.org/CNI/wg.docs/architecture/lynch.overview.txt]

Lynch, Clifford A. (1994). - Rethinking the integrity of the scholarly record in the networked information age. - In: Educom review, 29(2).

Lynch, Clifford A. (1995). - The Z39.50 Protocol in plain English.

Lynch, Clifford A., and Preston, C. M. (1992). - Describing and classifying networked information resources. In: Electronic networking: research applications and policy Vol., 2(1):13-23.

Madson, O. (1994). - International Standard Bibliographic Description for Computer Files (ISBD(CF). - In: International Cataloguing and Bibliographic Control, 23, April/June, 2, 37.

Malinconico, S.M. - The use of electronic documents in libraries. - Paper presented at the 61st IFLA General Conference. - [http://www.nlc-bnc.ca/ifla/ifla61/61-mals.htm].

Martin, Harry S. III and Curtis Kendrick (1993). - A user-centered view of document delivery and interlibrary loan.
[http://www.nlc-bnc.ca/documents/libraries/resource-sharing/ill.txt]

Mitchell, Maurice, and Laverna M. Saunders. (1991). - The virtual library: an agenda for the 1990s. In: Computers in libraries, 11(4), 8 - 11.

Morgan, Eric Lease (1994). - The World-Wide Web and Mosaic: An overview for librarians. - In: Public-access computer systems review, 5(6), 5-26. [gopher://info.lib.uh.edu:70/00/articles/e-journals/uhlibrary/pacsreview/v5/n6/morgan.5n6].

Naylor, B. (1994). - On-Line text: delivery, usability and cost. An academic library viewpoint. - In: STM Newsletter 95(95), 9-15.

Neuman, B. Clifford (1992), Prospero: a tool for organizing Internet resources. - In: Electronic networking: research, applications and policy, Vol. 2, No. 1, Spring.

Nicholson, Dennis (1994a). - CATRIONA Project: context and model. - Submitted to LIS-link@mailbase.ac.uk..

Nicholson, Dennis (1994b). - CATRIONA: general assumptions. [http://www.bubl.bath.ac.uk/BUBL/catriona.html].

North American Interlibrary Loan & Document Delivery Project (1994). - Overview & vision. [http://www.nlc-bnc.ca/documents/libraries/resource-sharing/naildd1.txt].

Nürnberg, P.J. (1995). - Digital libraries: issues and architectures. - Paper presented at Digital Libraries 95. - [http://csdl.tamu.edu/DL95/papers/nuernberg/nuernberg.html].

Obraczka, Katia, Peter B. Danzig and Shih-Hao Li (1993). - Internet resource discovery services. - In: Computer, September:8-22.

Olsen, J. (1994). - Electronic journals: implications for scholars. - In: STM Newsletter 92(92), 6-17.

Olson, N.B. (1995). - Cataloging Internet resources, a manual and practical guide. -Dublin, Ohio: OCLC Online Computer Library Center, Inc. - ISBN: 1-55653-189-3. - [http://www.oclc.org/oclc/man/9256cat/toc.htm].

Olvey, L.S. (1995) - Library networks and electronic publishing. - In: Information services and use, (15), 39-47.

Omvlee, Jenny (1993). - De 'klant op afstand' nader bekeken. Gebruikersonderzoek bij de Bibliotheek van de TU Delft. - In: Open, 25(7/8), 273-277.

Oorschot, H. van (1994). - Strijd om standaard elektronische documenten. - In: EMNET(5), 9-10.

Pabbruwe, H. (1994). - Publishing without publishers?. - In: STM Newsletter 94(94), 18-19.

Peters, Paul Evan. (1993). - Internet information access and delivery: key concepts, tools, strategies, and issues.

Pettengill, P. ; Arango, G. (1995). - Four lessons learned from managing World Wide Web digital libraries. - Paper presented at Digital Libraries 95. - [http://csdl.tamu.edu/DL95/papers/pettengill/pettengill.html].

Postel, J. (editor) Internet Architecture Board, Network Working Group (1994).- Internet official Protocol Standards. Request for Comments:1720.

Price-Wilkin, J. (1994). - Using the World-Wide Web to deliver complex electronic documents: implications for libraries. - In: Public-access computer systems review, 5(3), 5-21.

Roes, H. (1994). - De opkomst van het elektronische tijdschrift. - In: EMNET(5), 7-9.

Rosenfeld, Louis B. (1994).- Guides, clearinghouses, and value-added repacking: some thoughts on how librarians can improve the Internet. - In: Reference services review, 22(4), 11-16.

Rothenberg, Jeff (1995). - Ensuring the longevity of digital documents. - In: Scientific American, 24-29.

Schwartz, M. F., Emtage, A., Kahle, B. and Neuman, B. C. (1992). - A comparison of Internet resource discovery approaches. - In: Computing systems, 5(4)461 - 493.

Scott, Peter (1992). - Using HYTELNET to access Internet resources. In: Public-access computer systems review, 3(4):15-21.

Sha, V. (1995). - Guidelines for cataloguing Internet resources. - [http://lawlib.wuacc.edu/listproc/intercat/feb95/msg00008.html].

Sha, V. (1995). - Internet resources for cataloging. - HTML version 2.0, 15 September 1995. - [http://asa.ugl.lib.edu/chdocs/libcat/libcat.htm].

Smoot, Carl-Mitchell and Quarterman, John S. (1993). - Practical Internetworking with TCP/IP and UNIX. Addison-Wesley Publishing Company.

Sollins, K. & Masinter, L. Network Working Group (1994). - Functional requirements for uniform resource locators. Request for Comments:1737.

Steele, Mary. - CATRIONA Model: Cataloguing and retrieval over networks.

Sugimoto, S. e.a. (1995). - Enhancing usability of network-based library information system: experimental studies of a user interface for OPAC and of a collaboration tool for library services. - Paper presented at Digital Libraries 95. - [http://csdl.tamu.edu/DL95/papers/sugimoto/sugimoto.html].

Surfnet (1994). - SURFdoc: storing, accessing and processing electronic documents: report of the implementation phase. - [ftp://ftp.nic.surfnet.nl/surfnet/projects/surfdoc/report-implementationphase-en.txt].

Surfnet (1994). - survey of projects and services in document delivery. - [ftp://ftp.nic.surfnet.nl/surfnet/projects/docdel/report-03-en.txt].

Swanekamp, J. (1994). - Interactive multimedia: issues for bibliographic control. - Paper presented at the Seminar on cataloging Digital Documents, Washington, Library of Congress, October 1994. - [http://lcweb.loc.gov/catdir/semdigdocs/joan.html].

Sy, Karen J. (1993).- The NII: what does it mean for libraries? (1993). - In: The CPSR Newsletter, 11(2), Summer 1993.

Taemin Kim Park (1994). - Toward a theory of user-based relevance: a call for a new paradigm of inquiry. - In: Journal of the American Society for Information Science, 45(3), 135-141.

Taylor, Robert S. (1986). - On the study of information use environments. - In: ASIS '86 Proceeding of the 49th ASIS Annual Meeting, 23, 331-334.

Technische problemen van het World-Wide Web op dit moment. (1995). In: EMNET(6), 2-3.

Theise, Eric S. (1994). - Curling up to universal resource locators.
[gopher://gopher.well.sf.ca.us:70/00/matrix/internet/curling.up.02].

Treloar, Andrew. (1993). - Towards a user-centred categorisation of Internet access tools. - In: Proceedings of Networkshop `93, Melbourne.
[FTP://ftp.unimelb.edu.au//pub/networkshop93/infores/treloar.txt]

Treloar, Andrew (1994). - The Internet as an information management technology: New tools, new paradigms and new problems. - Victoria: School of Computing and Mathematics, Deakin University, Rusden
[http://www.deakin.edu.au/people/aet/]

Truesdell, Cheryl, B. (1994). - Is access a viable alternative to ownership? A review of access performance. In Ann Arbor, MI (Ed.), - In: Journal of academic librarianship (pp. 200-206).

Turner, F. (1995). - An overview of the Z39.50 information retrieval standard. - (UDT Occasional paper, 3).
[http://www.nlc-bnc.ca/ifla/VI/5/op/udtop3.htm].

Turner, W. Network Working Group (1994). - The document architecture for the Cornell Digital Library. Request for Comments: 1691.

US National Commission on Libraries and Information Science. (1992). - Report to the Office of Science and Technology Policy on library and information services' roles in the National Research and Education Network. November 13, 1992.

Van House, N. (1995). - User needs assessment and evaluation for the UC Berkely Electronic Environmental Library Project: a preliminary report. - Paper presented at Digital Libraries 95. -
[http://csdl.tamu.edu/DL95/papers/vanhouse/vanhouse.html].

Verstraaten, R.E.C en Knippenberg, H.M. (1995). - Hoe wordt de tijdschriftencollectie gebruikt?. Een onderzoek bij een wetenschappelijke instituutsbibliotheek. - In: Open, 27(6), 187-190.

Vickery, J. (1995). - Acquisitions in an electronic age: building the foundations for access. - Paper presented at the 61st IFLA General Conference. -
[http://www.nlc-bnc.ca/ifla/IV/ifla61/61-vicj.htm].

Vizine-Goetz; Diane, Jean Godby and Mark Bendig (1994). - Spectrum: a Web-based tool for describing electronic resources. - Dublin, Ohio: OCLC.

Voorbij, Henk (1993). - Bibliotheekgebruikers en kosten/baten afwegingen. - In: Open, 25(4), 137-141.

Wahlde, B. von (1995). - Access vs. ownership: a SUNY University Center Libraries study of the economics of document delivery. - Paper presented at the 61st IFLA General Conference. -
[http://www.nlc-bnc.ca/ifla/IV/ifla61/61-wahb.htm].

Wahlde, Barbara von, and Nancy Schiller. (1993). - Creating the virtual library: strategic issues. In: The virtual library: visions and realities. Edited by Laverna M. Saunders. - Westport, CT: Meckler, 15 - 46.

Wainwright, E. (1994). - Networked library applications: toward a coherent strategy.

Waldstein, R. - Z39.50 resources: a pointer page. -
[http://ds.internic.net/z3950/z3950.html].

Waugh, Andrew. - Where are the network applications? - Carlton: CSIRO Division of Information Technology.

Weibel, S. ; Godby, J. ; LeVan, R. (1995). - An architecture for scholarly publishing in the World Wide Web. - Dublin, Ohio: Office of research, OCLC inc. - [http://www.ncsa.uiuc.edu/sdg/it94/proceedings/Pub/weibel/weibel_www_paper.html].

Weibel, S. ; Godby, J. ; Miller, E. (1995). - OCLC/NCSA Metadata Workshop report. - [http://www.oclc.org:5046/conferences/metadata/dublin_core_report.html].

Weibel, S. (1994). - Existing Library standards and the evolution of uniform recource characteristics. - San Jose, Cal.: IETF URI working group.

Weider, Chris and Peter Deutsch (1994b). - Uniform Resource Names: Internet draft. [FTP://nic.nordu.net/Internet-drafts/draft-ietf-uri-resource-names-02.txt]

Weider, Chris and Peter Deutsch (1994a). - A vision of an integrated Internet information service: Internet draft. [FTP://nic.merit.edu/documents/Internet-drafts/draft-ietf-iiir-vision-02.txt]

Werf, T. v.d. (1994a). - Cataloguing the Internet. - The Hague: Koninklijke Bibliotheek.

Werf, Titia van der (1994). - InfoServices: cooperation between the national research network service and the National Library in the Netherlands. - In: Journal of information networking, 2(1), 13-22.

Willis, Katherine; Alexander, Ken, Gosling, William, A., etc. (1994). - TULIP - The university licensing program: experiences at the University of Michigan. - In: Serials review, 20(3), 39-48.

Woodward, H. ; Rowland, F. (1994). - ELVYN: the delivery of an electronic version of a journal from the publisher to libraries. - In: JUGL 94 Conference, 22 June. - [http://info.lut.ac.uk/departments/dils/Elvyn/join.html].

Zhao, Dian, G. (1994). - The ELINOR electronic library system. - In: Electronic library, 12(5), 289-294.

The Communities research and development information service
CORDIS

A vital part of your programme's dissemination strategy

CORDIS is the information service set up under the VALUE programme to give quick and easy access to information on European Community research programmes. It is available free-of-charge online via the European Commission host organization (ECHO), and now also on a newly released CD-ROM.

CORDIS offers the European R&D community:

— a comprehensive up-to-date view of EC R&TD activities, through a set of databases and related services,

— quick and easy access to information on EC research programmes and results,

— a continuously evolving Commission service tailored to the needs of the research community and industry,

— full user support, including documentation, training and the CORDIS help desk.

The CORDIS Databases are:

**R&TD-programmes – R&TD-projects – R&TD-partners – R&TD-results
R&TD-publications – R&TD-comdocuments – R&TD-acronyms – R&TD-news**

Make sure your programme gains the maximum benefit from CORDIS

— Inform the CORDIS unit of your programme initiatives,

— contribute information regularly to CORDIS databases such as R&TD-news, R&TD-publications and R&TD-programmes,

— use CORDIS databases, such as R&TD-partners, in the implementation of your programme,

— consult CORDIS for up-to-date information on other programmes relevant to your activities,

— inform your programme participants about CORDIS and the importance of their contribution to the service as well as the benefits which they will derive from it,

— contribute to the evolution of CORDIS by sending your comments on the service to the CORDIS Unit.

For more information about contributing to CORDIS, contact the DG XIII CORDIS Unit

Brussels	*Luxembourg*
Ms I. Vounakis	M. B. Niessen
Tel. +(32) 2 299 0464	Tel. +(352) 4301 33638
Fax +(32) 2 299 0467	Fax +(352) 4301 34989

To register for online access to CORDIS, contact:

ECHO Customer Service
BP 2373
L-1023 Luxembourg
Tel. +(352) 3498 1240
Fax +(352) 3498 1248

If you are already an ECHO user, please mention your customer number.

European Commission

EUR 16905 — Knowledge models for networked library services

J. S. Mackenzie Owen, A. Wiercx

Luxembourg, Office for Official Publications of the European Communities

1996 — IX, 190 pp. — 21.0 x 29.7 cm

Libraries in the information society series

ISBN 92-827-5838-9

Price (excluding VAT) in Luxembourg: ECU 16

The study on Knowledge models for networked library services is published as an addition to the series in parallel with another study report on Open distance learning in public libraries (EUR 16904). Both are considered as key contributions to the expanding role of public libraries in the networked environment.

The principal objective of the knowledge models study has been to investigate the library's evolving role in the mediation process, combining collection-based resources with access to external documents of various types. In this context, it provides guidelines for librarians and library users wishing to make use of new models for acquisition, lending and reference based on integrated access to networked functions.